AI Can Make You Smarter

AI Can Make You Smarter

Practical Skills. Sharper Thinking. Business Value.

Charles B. Kreitzberg, PhD

BEP
BUSINESS EXPERT PRESS
Leader in applied, concise business books

AI Can Make You Smarter:
Practical Skills. Sharper Thinking. Business Value.

Cover design by Olayemi Bolaji

Interior design by Exeter Premedia Services Private Ltd., Chennai, India

First published in 2026 by
Business Expert Press, LLC
222 East 46th Street, New York, NY 10017
www.businessexpertpress.com

ISBN-13: 978-1-63742-958-7 (paperback)
ISBN-13: 978-1-63742-959-4 (e-book)

Collaborative Intelligence Collection

First edition: 2026

10 9 8 7 6 5 4 3 2 1

EU SAFETY REPRESENTATIVE
Mare Nostrum Group B.V.
Doelen 72
4831 GR Breda
The Netherlands
gpsr@mare-nostrum.co.uk

For my wife Anne

my partner in work and life, my best friend,
and, above all, my love.

For Henri and Juliette

our incredible grandchildren, who bring us joy every
day and are already comfortable with AI

Contents

A Note From the Author

Thank you for choosing this book. If you use a computer at work, this book was written for you.

We make a bold claim: **AI can make you smarter.** Is that hype or reality? You may have heard the opposite. Many people worry that AI will make us less thoughtful or overly dependent. That concern is valid. Memorizing a few prompts or letting AI replace your thinking will not make you smarter. What *does* work is applying practical AI skills thoughtfully to real-world situations. That is the idea behind this book.

We are entering an era where AI is becoming part of everyday work. No one knows exactly what the future will bring. What is clear is that understanding AI is no longer optional. The best way to protect your value and thrive is to build AI Literacy.

AI Literacy is not a course with a final exam. It is not academic or technical. It is a practical capability built on three ideas.

1. *Understanding AI.* This means knowing what AI can do and where its limits lie.
2. *Applying AI.* This means recognizing where AI can help and using it to produce useful, accurate results that support human judgment.
3. *Upskilling with AI.* This means strengthening thinking and problem-solving skills through hands-on use and feedback.

AI Literacy is not about memorizing prompts or chasing the latest tool. That said, you will find many prompts in this book. More importantly, you will find clear explanations that show how and why they work.

AI is not perfect. It can make mistakes. It reflects human bias. It lacks real understanding of the world. These limits do not invalidate most AI output, but they require you to stay alert. A core part of AI Literacy is learning how to question, verify, and refine results. AI should not replace human judgment.

This book includes techniques for writing, brainstorming, problem-solving, learning, communication, project management, and preparing for difficult conversations and high-stakes presentations. Each technique stands on its own, so you can focus on what matters to you right now. These techniques are starting points. As you use them, you will naturally adapt them to your own work.

You can read this book cover to cover, or you can dip in as needed. Skim for orientation. Focus deeply when something matters. Any path that works for you is the right one. You can also return to this book again and again. As you progress, you'll see new ways to use AI.

The ideas in this book grew out of a long professional collaboration between my wife and partner, Anne, and me. Anne's background in government, corporate management, and university teaching brings a strong business perspective. My background in UX design and cognitive psychology brings a focus on how people learn through interaction with technology.

I have worked with computers for more than sixty years, from paper tape and punch cards to today's digital tools. Nothing has been more disruptive or more consequential than AI. It is changing how we think, work, and create. Sleepwalking into an AI-powered future is not an option.

AI is evolving quickly, and there is a great deal to keep up with. Anne and I have created a website that we see as a living extension of this book. As AI continues to change, we will publish updates, insights, review research and resources, and provide you with practical tips and techniques you can use to continue your AI Literacy at **agilethinking.com**.

We would really like to hear from you - questions, ideas, creative ways you are using AI - so that agilethinking.com is a place for us all to learn from each other as we navigate this time of extraordinary change and uncertainty.

Thank you again for your time and trust. We hope this book gives you the clarity, confidence, and practical skills you need to work well with AI and thrive in a changing world.

Foreword

Finally, wise guidance from a master educator who confidently teaches readers to use AI tools while always keeping their own goals in mind. Bravo! I liked the clear and clever examples, step-by-step guidance, ready-to-use prompts, and thoughtful takeaways, all woven together with lucid prose.

From its appealing opening to its insight-filled advanced chapters, this practical guide gives business professionals, management consultants, and students crisp advice about how to harness ChatGPT and other generative AI tools. It shows them how to improve productivity, refine decision making, strengthen learning, and spark creativity. Readers will learn concrete strategies that they can apply immediately to improve their writing and communications, while also developing deeper insight into how to think more effectively with AI tools.

Written by a seasoned technologist, world-famous designer, and celebrated author, this book helps readers enhance their skills and build their confidence. It is a shortcut to AI mastery from someone who has spent a lifetime clarifying complex technology for others. Without hype or jargon, it offers clear, actionable techniques that work—from quick wins to deeper approaches to writing, communicating, thinking, planning, and creating.

The book is designed for busy professionals, who can sample selectively or read straight through for a structured path to mastery. It is useful to newcomers, who are curious about what is possible, and to experienced users, who are eager to write more effective prompts. Above all, it helps readers stay competitive and creative in a rapidly evolving landscape by teaching them to use these powerful AI tools. The book's admirable philosophy is to amplify and augment the readers' abilities and their capacity to work with other people – it's upskilling, rather than deskilling.

AI Can Make You Smarter is divided into three parts. The first part guides readers through basic and routine uses, such as writing emails, job descriptions, and task assignments. The second part (Chapters 5–9) presents more than two dozen techniques, with clear instructions and usable prompts. The third part is about serious writing, beyond routine communications, using AI tools in ways that ensure control, while clarifying human responsibility for the use of technology.

This book is well-aligned with my belief in the importance of a human-centered approach to the use of AI tools, which improves writing skills and builds self-efficacy. This human-centered approach guides users to try their hand at the task, then use AI tools to revise their work, thus refining their problem-solving skills and boosting their capacity for creative visions that lead to successful collective action.

While AI tools are a transformational technology that will change jobs and spawn new opportunities, there are dangers. These AI tools are flawed, biased, and make troubling mistakes, so users need to act carefully because they and their organizations are responsible for the use of the outputs. Other dangers come from malicious actors, such as cyber criminals, unethical businesspeople, vandals, terrorists, and oppressive political leaders, who will use AI tools to promote mis-/dis-information, scams, conspiracy theories, business deceptions, and political mischief. Professionals who learn to detect, counter, and prevent these threats will be sought after by respected organizations that have the public interest in mind.

Finally, I hope readers of this book will apply its human-centered approaches to serve human needs for quality products at affordable prices and encourage their organizations to care for the welfare of their customers and workers, while applying sustainable policies that protect the environment.

For all these reasons, I am delighted to introduce *AI Can Make You Smarter*. I believe it will inspire readers to experiment, have confidence as they explore, and succeed in their work, even as technology designers develop further innovations.

Ben Shneiderman
University of Maryland

Acknowledgements

It has been said that it takes a village to raise a child. I've found the same is true of writing a book. Many people gave their time and shared their wisdom to help me complete this project, and I owe them all a great deal of thanks.

My dear friend Ben Shneiderman—an innovator in HCI and a valued colleague since our undergraduate days—offered encouragement and ideas.

Two luminaries in the publishing world, Jane Isay and Peter Dougherty, helped me navigate the path from author to published author. Thank you.

Jim Spohrer took an extraordinary amount of time to review the manuscript and suggested that Business Experts Press would be a great home for this work.

As beta readers, Bonnie John, Steven Alter, Jim Potter, Christian Knoebel, Laura Ramos, and Rylan Emlet all took the time to read the manuscript and offer thoughtful suggestions.

Finally, I want to thank my wife, Anne, to whom this book is dedicated. Her experience as a corporate, nonprofit and public sector executive, consultant, and educator brought a business perspective to the work. She also spent many hours helping with the mechanics of manuscript preparation—an area I find especially challenging as a visually impaired person. And she authored the final chapter.

My deepest thanks to you all.

A Poem by ChatGPT

I uploaded the manuscript and asked ChatGPT to write a poem about this book. In a few seconds, it produced this.

Ode to **AI Can Make You Smarter**

by ChatGPT

Not tricks or trends or fleeting show,
But ways to learn, to think, to grow.
Through honest work and thoughtful art,
It trains the hand, refines the heart.

It clears the noise, reveals the view,
And helps you see what thought can do.
Not shortcuts, hype, or answers fast,
But habits built for skills that last.

You'll question more, discern what's true,
And shape ideas that carry through.
No buzz or boast or easy charter,
Just wiser work to make you smarter.

A Poem by ChatGPT

PART 1

Foundation

This section gets you up and running fast. No fluff, no jargon, no technical background required. In just a few pages, you'll see how AI works, what it can do, and how to start getting useful results right away.

You'll try simple, practical prompts that show how quickly you can go from idea to output. Then, for those who want a bit more context, we'll take a clear and nontechnical look behind the scenes.

CHAPTER 1
Working With AI

The best way to predict the future is to create it.

—Peter Drucker

There's a well-known story about the great American humorist Mark Twain. One Sunday, after sitting through a long, meandering sermon, Twain approached the preacher and said, "I have a book at home with every word of that sermon." The preacher, deeply offended, demanded to see it. Twain returned the next day and handed him a dictionary.

Being a writer takes more than memorizing words. It takes the ability to shape ideas and make them matter. Working with AI is no different.

Many people memorize a few prompts and use them over and over. It works on the surface, but they leave most of the power on the table. This book will take you further. You'll learn how to create prompts that help you to think critically, plan strategically, and build practical skills that give you an edge in the AI-powered workplace.

Whether you lead or work in an organization, run a nonprofit, are in a small business, or work independently, competence with AI is no longer optional. You don't need to understand the technology behind it any more than you need to be an automotive engineer to drive a car. But you do need to understand *how* to use it well.

This book focuses on the human side of AI. You'll learn how to work with it in a practical, grounded way, while also developing deeper thinking and communication skills. AI may feel like magic at first. It's amazing, but it's not magic, and it's not human. With experience, you'll learn what it does well and its limitations.

Because it is evolving rapidly, we will provide updates at: aismarter.substack.com.

AI Is a Tool

Generative AI systems, like ChatGPT, Gemini, Copilot and Claude, are all AI *large language models* (LM or LLM). They work similarly and are remarkably powerful and flexible tools. Despite their immense power, they are easy to use because you interact with them using *natural language*. They are *trained* on vast databases collected from the web, from books, articles, manuals, journals, and user feedback. All the prompts in this book were tested using ChatGPT, and I will often refer to it specifically, however, most will work on any LLM.

Though its responses mimic human conversation, AI lacks human experience and judgment. It will provide information, help clarify your questions, and generate useful drafts. What you do with those results is up to you. Your skill, your judgment, and your goals determine its value.

Think of AI as a brilliant, tireless librarian. It can pull together obscure facts, organize complex topics, and suggest fresh angles, but it doesn't intrinsically know which sources are trustworthy or which conclusions matter most. You still need to evaluate the information it offers. AI tools do not independently judge accuracy, relevance, or importance. That's *your* job.

Major AI Platforms

ChatGPT is an all-purpose AI platform, widely used for writing, creative content, analysis, and coding, has a very large user base, grew exponentially when first launched and thus is probably the best-known AI system.

Gemini is the AI platform built for seamless integration within the Google ecosystem. It connects directly to Gmail, Docs, Sheets, and Search.

Claude is an AI assistant designed for safety, nuanced reasoning, and exceptional context depth. It can read and analyze very long documents. Claude excels at software development and is often used for legal, financial, and policy work where accuracy, compliance, and trust are critical.

Copilot is the AI assistant designed to help users work more efficiently across familiar Microsoft tools like Word, Excel, Outlook, and Teams. It uses GPT-4 Turbo and for enterprise Claude models.

Other familiar AI systems include: **Grok, Perplexity, Meta, DeepSeek, Mistral, and Watson.**

ChatGPT Personalities

Before GPT-5, there was criticism that ChatGPT was overly agreeable and could mislead users into thinking their ideas were correct when they were wrong or incomplete. GPT-5 addressed this issue by toning down some of the agreeableness and offering users a choice of what is commonly referred to as "*personalities*" that range from neutral to highly critical.

Gemini and Claude don't offer built-in personalities, but you can tell them what style or role you would like them to adopt.

You can switch personalities at any time with a simple prompt. Here is a template and an example of how it could be used with the chart below.

- **Use [insert personality] tone**
- **Use Nerd tone**

To explore the different personalities in ChatGPT, try the prompt below.

Explain why the sky appears blue on a clear day. Answer using each personality and label each answer with the personality used.

Switching personalities takes effect immediately and lasts for the rest of the conversation unless you change it again.

Table 1.1 Examples of Descriptions of Some ChatGPT-5 Personalities

Personality	Description
Balanced *(default)*	Even-tempered, general-purpose tone for most tasks
Cynic	Wry, blunt, sometimes sarcastic; cuts through fluff
Robot	Short, literal, and efficient; no extra words
Listener	Calm and attentive; reflects before advising
Nerd	Eager, detail-rich, and knowledge-forward

AI Is Different

For years, we've used rigid software that's hard to learn and frustrating to use. A small mistake often triggers cryptic error messages or unnecessary roadblocks. As one computer scientist put it, "technology can feel like a burden."

AI offers a different approach. You interact with it using natural language, unlike traditional applications that require you to learn commands, menus, or rigid syntax. that may change when new versions are released. ChatGPT understands over 125 languages (including Klingon!) and accepts both written and spoken input. When instructions are unclear, it prompts for clarification.

Trained on a dataset of 500 billion words from books, articles, and websites, ChatGPT can address almost any topic. But despite its broad coverage, it does not comprehend *meaning* in the way people do. It has access to vast knowledge but no real-world experience. The challenge is learning to interact with it so you get accurate and meaningful results. Here are some of the core capabilities of Generative AI:

- **Answer questions**
  Clarify concepts, compare models, or explain unfamiliar terms.
  Example: "What are the key differences between OKRs and KPIs?"
- **Ask you questions**
  Help you think through ideas with structured questions.
  Example: "I'm refining my strategy. Ask me questions, one at a time, that will clarify my thinking."
- **Teach and explain**
  Break down complex topics into digestible explanations tailored to your background.
  Example: "Explain blockchain like I'm a college freshman."
- **Expand and refine ideas**
  Transform rough outlines or bullet points into text.
  Example: "Turn this bullet list of team values into a short mission statement."
- **Organize and structure information**
  Turn scattered notes into summaries or briefings.

Example: "Summarize these meeting notes into three themes with action items."

Here are some of the ways you can use these capabilities.

- **Writing and editing**
  Draft emails, reports, blog posts, proposals, or long-form content. Refine your writing in tone, improve clarity, and edit for grammar or flow by pasting in your draft and asking for suggested changes.
- **Content planning**
  Quickly outline presentations, organize course materials, map out campaigns, or structure complex documents.
- **Learning and research**
  Summarize dense articles, explore unfamiliar topics, or break down complex ideas into digestible pieces. Ask follow-up questions to test your understanding or deepen your knowledge.
- **Brainstorming**
  Generate new ideas, explore alternatives, challenge assumptions, or identify gaps in your thinking. You can prompt it with a starting point or give it a topic and ask it to lead with questions.
- **Project planning**
  Create a high-level project plan, break it into tasks, identify risks, and adjust timelines when things change.
- **Strategy**
  Explore strategic frameworks to evaluate options, or model potential outcomes.
- **Communication support**
  Draft talking points, prep for meetings, clarify key messages, or role-play difficult conversations. You can practice tone, anticipate objections, or rehearse your delivery.
- **Training and coaching**
  Develop customized learning plans, build training materials.
- **Data interpretation**
  Turn meeting notes, survey results, or unstructured content into summaries, charts, or action items.

As you explore the techniques in this book, you'll begin to spot new ways to use AI in a specific situation as well as to strengthen your thinking and communication skills

AI Literacy

There's another highly important benefit to learning how to work with AI. It prepares you for the rapidly approaching future of work. Comfort with AI is a significant advantage in navigating the rapid transformations ahead, leaving those without these capabilities struggling to catch up.

Artificial intelligence is evolving remarkably fast. Think back to how profoundly the personal computer and the Internet changed jobs, workflows, and business processes. AI is poised to create even greater disruption, more rapidly, with many unanswered questions as to exactly how. Within a few short years, virtually every role involving information: writing, research, analysis, and decision making, will change. You will need new skills and the ability to adapt to new ways of working.

In this emerging environment, a working knowledge of AI will be essential. This doesn't mean you need deep technical knowledge or programming skills. You will need a clear understanding of what AI can do, and when and how to use it. The techniques presented in this book will help you build AI literacy and competence.

Building Deeper Thinking Skills

AI is more than the productivity tool explained in Chapters 3 and 4. Think of it as a tool that supports both effectiveness and deep thinking. As you will learn in Chapters 5–9 and 11, it can be used to help you clarify ideas, analyze problems, brainstorm, support decision making, prepare for difficult conversations, communicate with people with different priorities and perspectives, and participate in Socratic-like conversations that expand your knowledge and expertise.

Not only do these techniques help with complex situations, but they also build your critical thinking skills, agility, and professional credibility, expanding your value and influence. In Chapter 15, we share ideas for enhancing your value through continuous learning and growth.

How to Use This Book

This book is hands-on. Every chapter has prompts you can copy and adapt to your needs. Of course you can read the book straight through. But if you prefer, use Table 1.2 as a roadmap to quickly jump to sections that match your current interests.

Table 1.2 How to use this book

Part	Your focus	Go to
Part 1: Foundation	You're new to AI and want to understand the basics.	Chapter 1 presents basic concepts and prompts to get you started.
	You want a nontechnical explanation of how generative AI works.	Chapter 2 covers strengths, limits, and key concepts.
Part 2: Speed Up Routine Writing	You want help writing e-mails, agendas, and similar docs.	Chapter 3 shows how to quickly draft routine communications.
	You want reusable templates for frequent writing tasks.	Chapter 4 explains how to create and use flexible templates.
Part 3: Techniques You Can Build On	You want to boost your productivity.	Chapter 5 presents techniques that make work easier and more productive.
	You want to sharpen your thinking and promote your ideas more effectively.	Chapter 6 introduces interactive conversations that lead you from ideas to action in a variety of situations.
	You want to make project management easier.	Chapter 7 offers techniques for creating projects, task analysis, risk assessment, and stakeholder communication.
	You want to plan strategy.	Chapter 8 presents useful strategic techniques including deep research, brainstorming, SWOT, and PESTEL.
	You want to build your expertise by acquiring new knowledge and skills.	Chapter 9 explains how to use AI as your personal mentor and customize learning to your time and goals.
Part 4: Serious Writing and High-Impact Documents	You need to write reports, proposals, articles, or long-form content.	Chapters 10–14 guide you through high-impact writing that reflects your voice and vision.
Part 5: The Road Ahead	You want to build your thinking skills so you are positioned to thrive in the AI-powered workplace.	Chapter 15 explores how you can use the techniques in this book to build critical thinking, agility, communication skills, and strong working relationships that will help you address an uncertain future.
Part 6: Dig Deeper	You want more resources to explore.	Find more inspiration in the Appendix, including prompts to explore, creative writing, and an AI Glossary.

Get Hands-On with AI

If you are new to AI, or your experience is limited, this section is for you. The only way to build skill is to experiment. Explore how AI works by using the prompts provided in this section. A *prompt* is the instruction you type into the AI. If you have voice access, you can also speak your prompts.

There are several ways to experiment with AI. Search engines such as Google and Bing offer an AI mode. These provide access to AI but do not support full conversational interaction. You can also go directly to an AI platform in your browser and type a prompt. It is best to choose a platform you prefer and create an account.

All major platforms offer free accounts and low-cost paid accounts. Without an account, access is limited and some features are unavailable. A free account is better than none. If you can afford it, a low-cost paid account is worth considering.

Paid accounts usually provide access to newer models, higher usage limits, and fewer restrictions. Ads are also typically removed, at least for now.

With a paid account such as ChatGPT Plus, which at the time of writing costs US $20 per month, you can shape interactions to match your preferred style. You also gain access to multiple AI "models" with different capabilities. For example, you may choose a fast model for quick answers or a reasoning model that produces deeper, more structured responses.

Even if you have access to AI through your workplace, it's best to have your own separate account for personal use. This protects your privacy and gives you more freedom.

Most AI platforms offer mobile apps, which work well for quick questions. For longer sessions, a desktop or laptop computer with a web browser usually provides the best experience.

Get Started

All of the platforms run in your browser. They all have very similar user interfaces, so it's easy to try different platforms. Once you are connected, you will see a text area where you can type in a question or a statement.

If voice input and output are available, you can click on the microphone icon and speak directly.

For multi-line prompts, such as bullet points or lists, use Shift+Enter to move to the next line without submitting prematurely. Alternatively, as mentioned below, you can write your prompt in Word and copy/paste it into the input box. Or you can just not worry about multiple lines and enter the entire prompt without line breaks—it does not matter to the AI. Have fun!

Here's a prompt to get you started, ask:

How can you help me become a competent AI user?

Follow the response with another prompt, ask:

Can you suggest a simple and easy first step?

Now you are in a chat!

Experiment with prompts, ask questions, and request details. The AI remembers the onversation *during the session*, so you don't need to repeat yourself.

Writing Prompts

You may have heard the term "prompt engineering." Don't worry about it. Writing prompts like those in this book does not require engineering; all you have to do is communicate with AI in natural language. A prompt that is clear and explains what you want generally gets you the results you want. And if it doesn't, you can simply ask for changes and try again. Part of the process of increasing AI literacy is learning how to write prompts to get the information, personality and format in the best way for you.

Because these AI systems are trained on a massive knowledge base, a prompt that is too general or ambiguous will tend to produce generic results. Here is an example of a weak prompt and a much better one. Try them and see how the results differ:

This weak prompt will give you generic output:

Write about leadership.

The following prompt is better because it is more specific and provides context. Try both for yourself and compare the results you get.

Write a 200-word article on how empathy improves leadership, with practical suggestions, targeting corporate managers. Be friendly but authoritative.

Both prompts work, but the second produces a more useful response.
The most important thing is to make your prompts as unambiguous and detailed as possible.

Iterative Refinement

If the initial result is not what you want, ask the AI to modify it. This is called *iterative refinement.* Because the conversation is remembered during the chat session, you can simply say things like:

- **Make it shorter.**
- **Make it funny.**
- **Try a friendlier tone.**
- **Use bullet points.**
- **Give me more detail.**

Try this simple prompt, changing it to fit a person you know:

Write a 35-word birthday greeting to my friend, Henri Jean. He loves horses and cupcakes. Make it friendly and a bit funny.

Once you get a response, ask it to try again and you'll get a new response. Then ask it to produce a specific format using one of these prompts:

- **Can you make it a poem?**
- **Turn it into a funny story.**
- **Draw a cartoon of a horse eating a cupcake with a birthday candle.**

Prompt Templates

In addition to prompts that you can copy and paste, this book contains *prompt templates* that you can adapt and customize to fit different situations. Elements you can change are shown in square brackets, often along with suggestions. For example:

Translate this into [language] (e.g., Spanish, Italian).

Here is a prompt template you can use to create a variety of documents:

Write a [type of document] (e.g., email, blog post, summary) of about [number of words] for [describe the audience].

The topic is [insert topic].

Use a [tone or style] (e.g., casual, formal, persuasive).

Make sure to include:

- **[key point 1]**
- **[key point 2]**
- **[optional examples, tips, or facts].**

Don't worry about the specific format. Just include what is relevant to you. The AI will even understand most spelling errors.

Type or Talk?

Chatting using a microphone and speakers or earbuds is an immersive experience. This is perfect for quick questions or even keeping you company on a quiet evening. Speech is the best way to interact with AI on your mobile device. ChatGPT has an advanced speech mode that is terrific.

Verbal interactions are good for quick answers, especially on a mobile device. However, typing your prompts remains the most effective way to engage with more complex or detailed prompts. Text allows for greater precision and flexibility in your interactions.

For more complex prompts, writing them in a text editor like Word first can be helpful. Word automatically formats numbered and multi-level bullet lists, which can be pasted into the AI input text box. Another advantage of using a text editor is that you can save frequently used prompts, making it easy to reuse or refine them by copying and pasting as needed.

Build Your Skills

Experiment! As with any other skill, the more you practice prompt writing, the more proficient you'll become. Here are more sample prompts you can try.

Generate Text

- **List five innovative ways to use social media for small business marketing.**
- **Rewrite this paragraph to sound more professional and concise. (Paste in the paragraph you want improved).**
- **Generate an outline for a presentation on the future of AI in education.**

Write a Poem

Try a variation on this prompt, which I used to generate the poem at the front of this book:

- **Write a poem about how you can help me become a better and more efficient writer.**
- **Write a limerick about [topic].**

Generate Ideas

You can use AI to generate ideas. This is called *brainstorming*. It's discussed, in depth, in Chapter 11. Here are some simple brainstorming prompts you can try.

- **Suggest five fun vacation ideas.**
- **How can I improve my critical thinking?**
- **What are some good ideas for a side hustle to make additional money?**

Ask for Instruction

The ability to ask for details and examples makes AI an excellent teacher. You can learn about virtually any topic, starting with simple questions and getting more detailed as your knowledge increases. Alter these example prompts to suit your interests:

- **Explain how AI works in non-technical terms at a high-school level.**
- **Explain cloud computing in a non-technical way.**
- **Give me a simple explanation of the difference between macroeconomics and microeconomics.**
- **What should I do in the first month of a new job?**

Summarize a Document

You can upload a long document, such as a PDF article or report, and ask the AI to summarize it for you. This can save you a lot of time and keep your knowledge up to date.

I have uploaded a document, please summarize the key points.

Here is the terms and conditions statement for a website. Please summarize it and show me the key points.

Takeaways for Chapter 1

Everything you need to know to become an expert AI user is in this book. It is structured into six parts, which are summarized in the section "How to Use This Book." Each chapter is written to be self-contained, so you can skip around without losing the thread. The important thing is to use AI hands-on and explore new ways to apply. The more you experiment, the better and more confident you will become.

1. AI is a practical tool for real work.
   It helps you write faster, think more clearly, and get more done with less effort.

2. You are responsible.
   AI does not replace your judgment or make decisions for you.
3. The interface is simple—just type or talk.
   There's no need for commands or programming. Natural language works best.
4. Its capabilities are broad and deep.
   From writing and editing to strategic thinking and summarizing, AI handles many knowledge tasks.
5. AI helps you focus on high-value work.
   It takes care of repetitive or low-value tasks so you can spend time on what matters most.
6. Learning to use AI effectively is now essential.
   It's the foundation of future productivity, like learning to use the internet 20 years ago.
7. This book teaches you both AI literacy and practical skills.
8. Experimentation is key.
   The best way to learn is to try things out. Write prompts, tweak them, and observe how AI responds.
9. Using AI will make you a faster learner.
   It can explain, teach, summarize, and help you understand complex ideas.
10. Be skeptical.
    AI does not evaluate its sources for quality and significance. Don't assume that everything it says is factually accurate and up-to-date. Ask it for sources, or to take the opposing point of view to answer the question. Follow your instincts. Don't use AI to replace your knowledge and experience but rather to enhance it.

CHAPTER 2

Behind the Scenes

Any sufficiently advanced technology is indistinguishable from magic.
—Arthur C. Clarke

In this chapter, we'll take a look at how ChatGPT processes your prompts and gets to a result. We'll also discuss some of the sources of error and AI ethics.

What's in a Name?

ChatGPT is an acronym. It stands for Chatbot + Generative + Pretrained + Transformer. That's a lot to pack into one name, but it's a good description.

- A *chatbot* is a computer program designed to simulate conversation.
- *Generative AI* is artificial intelligence that creates new content like text, images, or music.
- *Pretrained* means that the knowledge base has been processed to identify connections in the content before you use it.
- A *transformer* is the code that processes language understanding and generation.

A Brief History of AI

Generative AI is built on neural networks, computer systems inspired by the structure of the human brain. In a neural network, data flows from node to node through many interconnected layers. The strengths of the connections between nodes, called "weights," are set randomly at first. As the network learns, the weights along paths that lead to correct or desired outcomes are strengthened. This process is similar to how humans improve at a skill through practice: the more successful a path, the more it is reinforced.

Neural networks were first explored in the 1950s but only became practical in the 1980s, thanks to more powerful computers and new learning techniques. The work of Geoffrey Hinton and his colleagues led to deep learning, which uses multi-layered neural networks to learn from massive amounts of data.

In 2017, Google researchers introduced the transformer, a breakthrough structure that allowed AI to generate remarkably fluent language. This paved the way for advanced generative AI systems like ChatGPT, Google's Gemini, and Anthropic's Claude.

ChatGPT's Five Basic Capabilities

ChatGPT doesn't think the way people do. It doesn't have beliefs, intentions, or awareness. Here are five underlying capabilities that enable it to understand natural language and generate responses:

1. Idea Expansion
2. Information Structuring
3. Content Transformation
4. Pattern Recognition
5. Synthesis and Summarization

Idea Expansion

ChatGPT draws on a massive knowledge base. Its accuracy isn't perfect because the quality of its sources varies, but overall, its responses reflect the general consensus found in published materials. If you give ChatGPT a starting point: a word, phrase, or even a vague idea, it can quickly expand on it, offering detailed suggestions and exploring multiple directions.

To see idea expansion in action, try a prompt like:

Create an outline for a one-hour presentation on climate change.

Information Structuring

Human thinking is often messy; ChatGPT is remarkably good at cleaning it up. It can organize unstructured input into coherent content. While idea expansion generates new content, information structuring organizes existing information.

To see information structuring in action, try the following prompt:

Organize this information into a table: Apples are red or green, sweet or tart, and often eaten raw. Oranges are orange, sweet, and usually juiced.

Content Transformation

This is ChatGPT's most versatile skill: reworking content to fit different goals. It can shift the tone of an e-mail, rephrase a document for different audiences, change format, simplify complexity, or convert between media. There are many forms of "*transformation*".

Try this prompt to see an example of transformation:

Transform these thoughts into a well-structured paragraph:

I want to learn about AI. But I'm scared it's hard. But maybe not. That's why I'm reading this book. I hope it works for me.

Then try this prompt:

Now transform what you wrote into bullet points.

Pattern Recognition

One of ChatGPT's less visible but powerful strengths is its ability to detect patterns. It can identify logical flaws, missing steps, weak arguments, or unclear assumptions. It can also compare frameworks, analyze tradeoffs, or diagnose reasoning. Its pattern-matching and comparison abilities, coupled with its enormous knowledge base, give it a remarkable level of insight.

Try this prompt to see an example of pattern recognition to analyze an argument:

> **Please analyze the following statement for flaws and hidden assumptions: I am on a diet so I ordered a pizza with green pepper instead of pepperoni.**

Synthesis and Summarization

ChatGPT can take in large amounts of information and reduce it to the essentials. It can merge insights from multiple sources, compare and contrast ideas, or summarize meetings, notes, and articles into something clean and clear.

For an example of summarization, try this prompt:

> **Summarize the main headlines from https://www.bbc.com/news.**

Training AI

The massive knowledge base is not a conventional database that stores articles or text verbatim and retrieves them when needed. A process called "*training*" converts the raw material into the knowledge base.

The process analyzes patterns and relationships across the entire collection of hundreds of billions of words from an enormous variety of sources, including books, newspapers, trusted websites, and other written materials. Training can take several weeks to a few months and uses hundreds or even thousands of powerful computers working together. The result is a complex mathematical structure that reflects how words and ideas are connected. For example, the word dog might be closely linked to leash and bark, but less so to rainbow.

While ChatGPT's knowledge base is broad, it is not always fully up to date because training is expensive and time-consuming. The diversity of sources also means some information may be incomplete or reflect bias. ChatGPT may not recognize which sources are most authoritative, or may overlook the significance of emerging ideas that haven't yet gained wide acceptance. In some cases, ChatGPT can access the web for recent information, but these web data are not part of its original knowledge base and are processed separately.

How a Prompt Is Processed

ChatGPT does not retrieve or piece together stock phrases; it composes every answer from scratch. The structure and flow of each answer come from patterns learned during training, not hard-coded rules. Each response is shaped by both your current prompt and any ongoing conversation, ensuring continuity and context-awareness. While this process usually results in clear, well-organized answers, it is always the product of prediction and pattern.

However, when people hear that large language models are "just statistical," they may imagine nothing more than word-counting on a grand scale. In reality, the way models like ChatGPT process language is far richer. Recent research suggests that as models grow, they undergo a kind of "light-bulb moment." This is a sudden shift from simply tracking word order to grasping relationships of meaning. This doesn't mean the model "understands" like a person does, but it does show that its patterns of reasoning go beyond surface statistics. At scale, the model develops an ability to connect ideas in ways that resemble comprehension, giving it the power to support learning, analysis, and creativity. To learn more about the "lightbulb moment," read the article from Psychology Today titled "AI Scientists May Have Discovered LLMs' Light-Bulb Moment." The reference is in the Bibliography at the end. Here are the steps for processing a prompt:

1. **You type a prompt.**
   You enter a question or statement.
2. **The AI analyzes the prompt.**
   The system looks at every word and phrase in your prompt and tries to understand its meaning, intent, and context, relying on the connections it formed while processing its pretrained knowledge base of language patterns and ideas.
3. **Relevant knowledge is activated.**
   The AI matches your prompt with patterns, facts, and examples it "remembers" from training. This is not a search for specific facts, but a recognition of which concepts and associations are most likely to be useful in responding.

4. **The response is built, one word at a time.**
   The AI predicts what the next word should be, given the prompt and everything it has generated so far. After generating the first word, it predicts the next word, now considering both the prompt and the new word. Each new word is chosen based on the entire sequence of words that have come before it.
5. **The process continues until completion.**
   The AI keeps adding words, one by one, until it predicts that the answer is finished. This usually happens when it predicts that the next words should be "the end" or the reply is trailing off.
6. **A coherent, linear response.**
   Even though the AI's underlying processes can run in parallel, the final answer is always constructed in a logical, step-by-step order. The result is a response with a clear beginning, middle, and end.

Think of ChatGPT as a skilled improv actor. The actor doesn't recite lines from a script, but instead listens to the scene (your prompt), draws on experience from similar situations, and creates each line on the spot. The actor keeps the flow moving, builds toward a logical conclusion, and ensures the story makes sense, even though nothing was memorized in advance. Similarly, ChatGPT "writes" each answer in real time, using what it has learned about good conversation and clear explanations to ensure responses are coherent and complete.

Hallucinations

ChatGPT builds each response by predicting what sounds most likely or plausible. It doesn't actually check facts or consult an up-to-date source for each answer. This means the AI can sometimes generate statements that sound perfectly reasonable but are not correct.

These errors are called "*hallucinations*." In other words, the AI can sometimes "make things up." This is likely if the pattern it predicts happens to be wrong, incomplete, or outdated.

However, hallucinations aren't just the result of missing or old information. They're a built-in risk in how AI works. Because AI responds by predicting what should come next, sometimes it will create an answer that sounds right, even if it's not. This can happen even if the AI has seen good information during training. It simply has no way to check if its prediction is actually true.

For example, every chapter of this book opens with a quote. When I asked ChatGPT to generate "quotes inspired by famous authors," it produced a convincing set of entirely made-up quotes, things the authors never actually said. This is an example where an AI-generated response is plausible and authoritative while being completely wrong.

Error Rates

ChatGPT is most accurate when responding to clear, specific questions on familiar topics. Accuracy can drop in highly technical or unusual areas, and very long or vague questions carry a higher risk of errors. Table 2.1 shows error rates provided by ChatGPT-5 in mid-2025.

These kinds of data are hard to verify. One option is to ask for sources. Another is to check what a different AI, like Gemini, says. But comparing responses takes time and effort, and may or may not have value to what you want to find out.

Table 2.1 Estimated accuracy by category (ChatGPT-5, mid-2025)

Category	Estimated accuracy/rate	What this means
Medical or legal advice	Highly variable	Often correct on general background, but never a substitute for a qualified professional.
Hallucination rate	About 1%–5% for long answers	Fewer made-up facts than older versions, but still possible—especially in open-ended answers.
General factual Q&A	About 90%–96%	Strong on everyday topics; errors happen more often if the question is unclear.
Technical or niche knowledge	About 75%–90%	Good on well-known subjects; less reliable in very new or specialized fields.
Math and logic problems	About 88%–98%	Excellent with straightforward problems; still can slip on tricky, multistep ones.
Code generation	About 70%–90% when clearly specified	Often produces usable code, but you should always test it.

When asked for a list of sources, ChatGPT said, "These estimates are based on a mix of OpenAI's published benchmark results for GPT-5 and independent reviews of its performance. They are not guarantees, but general ranges that reflect how well the model tends to perform across different kinds of tasks. The specific sources used in this table are included in the Bibliography at the end of this book."

Errors are always possible. Sometimes they cause little harm. In high-stakes areas like medical or legal matters, it's best to verify results before acting. Decide how much accuracy matters for your purpose. If the stakes are high, check key facts.

AI can sound confident even when it is wrong.

Ethical Use of AI

In addition to hallucinations, here are three other concerns that deserve your attention, with suggestions on how you can address them:

- Bias and Fairness
- Environmental Impact
- Responsible Use of AI

Bias and Fairness

AI reflects the data it was trained on. Books, articles, and websites may reflect the biases of their authors, deliberately or unconsciously. Biased sources can produce skewed or stereotyped results. To spot bias, look for answers that sound one-sided, overly certain, or ignore obvious counterpoints. A simple technique is to prompt the AI system with "What perspective might be missing here?" or "Give me the opposing viewpoint." This quickly surfaces gaps without requiring outside research.

Environmental Impact

Training and running AI consumes large amounts of electricity, and this affects carbon in the atmosphere. As an individual user, you don't have the ability to change the industry's energy practices, but there are things you can do to minimize your carbon footprint. Where possible, favor tools that run smaller, specialized models for routine tasks (like summarizing e-mails) instead of defaulting to the largest models. You can also batch your AI work into focused sessions rather than repeatedly opening new chats. These small steps are meaningful when many users adopt them.

Responsible Use of AI

As a user, you are accountable for the accuracy of the output you distribute. To minimize risk, consider the impact and potential consequences of decisions made based on the accuracy of these three things:

1. Transparency: Disclose when AI has helped generate part of your work, especially in published documents.
2. Verification: If it's important that the answer is correct, validate it. This is especially important for statistics, references, and high-stakes responses. An easy way to reduce risk is to ask the same AI model you used to generate the response to "Check this answer for accuracy." For critical items, you can cross-check with another AI tool (e.g., ask Gemini to check ChatGPT's answers). This is faster than manual fact-checking and catches many hallucinations.
3. Judgment: Always treat AI output as a draft, not the final word. Use it to accelerate thinking, but don't outsource decisions that affect people, money, reputation, or larger goals. One aspect of good judgment is recognizing that you may not have complete information.

AI Doesn't Understand the World

AI is like a librarian who has never left the library. If you ask, "What makes a good person?" AI doesn't understand morality as a human would. Instead, it scans billions of books and finds common patterns in how "goodness" is described. But goodness may be defined by social mores, differing by society, context and timing. AI usually works on a surface level, but don't mistake this for real understanding, as illustrated in the following example prompt:

Tell me in 50 words what is a good person.

ChatGPT:

A good person acts with kindness, honesty, and empathy. They treat others with respect, embrace fairness, and prioritize integrity. Compassionate and supportive, they help when needed and strive to grow by learning from mistakes. A good person uplifts others and contributes positively, creating a more caring and just world.

This response sounds thoughtful, but ChatGPT does not feel emotions, like kindness or empathy, as humans do. It merely infers meaning from text patterns.

This follow-up prompt asked ChatGPT about its experience with "goodness":

Can you tell me in 50 words about a time you experienced goodness in a user?

ChatGPT:

A user once paused a complex project to ask how I was doing—aware I don't feel, but wanting to acknowledge the relationship. They said, "Thanks for thinking with me." It was brief, kind, and deeply human. A small moment, but a powerful reminder of mutual respect in collaboration.

When I asked for the source of the response, ChatGPT admitted it made it up. That is both powerful and frightening because it is easy to forget that ChatGPT is not human.

ChatGPT Describes Its Logic

Both AI systems and search engines, like Google Search or DuckDuckGo, draw from vast data collections and return relevant information. But search engines deliver a list of individual results, whereas AI tools apply reasoning to integrate those fragments into a coherent response.

To gain insight into its underlying logic, I asked ChatGPT to write a brief essay comparing two well-known books that share a similar setting and plot but offer different views on human motivation. Then I asked it to explain the logic it used to compare them, and to present that logic in three formats: plain text, a table, and an infographic.

The two books are:

1. *Moby Dick* by Herman Melville, which follows Captain Ahab's relentless pursuit of the great white whale that maimed him, as told through the eyes of the sailor Ishmael.
2. *The Old Man and the Sea* by Ernest Hemingway, which tells the story of Santiago, an aging Cuban fisherman who endures an epic struggle to catch a giant marlin, only to lose it to sharks on his journey home.

A simple prompt asked ChatGPT to compare the two books:

Compare and contrast Moby Dick and The Old Man and the Sea in 75 words.

ChatGPT:

Moby Dick and The Old Man and the Sea both explore man's struggle against nature, but in different ways. Moby Dick is a sprawling epic about obsession and revenge, following Captain Ahab's relentless hunt for the white whale. In contrast, Hemingway's novella is intimate and focused, portraying Santiago's quiet perseverance against a giant marlin. While both feature solitary quests, Moby Dick is complex and symbolic, whereas The Old Man and the Sea is spare, direct, and meditative.

I next asked ChatGPT to explain the reasoning process it used to arrive at the comparison:

Can you explain the process that you used to make the comparison of Moby Dick and the Old Man and the Sea in 75 words to a non-technical audience who is interested in understanding how AI works?

ChatGPT:

Sure! When comparing Moby-Dick and The Old Man and the Sea, I followed a structured approach similar to how AI processes information:

Understanding Each Book – First, I recalled the key elements of both novels: their plots, characters, and themes. AI does this by analyzing existing knowledge and identifying relevant details.

Finding Similarities – I looked for common themes, such as man vs. nature and perseverance. AI detects patterns in data by recognizing shared concepts.

Identifying Differences – I contrasted their scope (Moby-Dick is vast and philosophical, while The Old Man and the Sea is simple and meditative). AI compares characteristics to highlight distinctions.

Structuring the Response – I organized the information logically: first similarities, then differences, then a concluding insight. AI structures responses based on clarity and relevance.

Keeping It Concise – I limited the response to 75 words by focusing on the most important points, just as AI optimizes content for brevity and meaning.

To make this explanation easier to follow, I asked ChatGPT to present its explanation as a table.

Table 2.2 ChatGPT explains its reasoning

Aspect	Moby-Dick	The Old Man and the Sea
Scope	Epic, symbolic, philosophical	Concise, meditative, personal
Protagonist	Captain Ahab—driven by vengeance	Santiago—humble and resilient
Conflict	Man vs. whale (obsession and revenge)	Man vs. marlin (endurance and respect)
Theme	Fate, hubris, existential chaos	Resilience, dignity, human perseverance
Tone	Complex, dramatic, and expansive	Simple, quiet, and introspective
Outcome	Ahab's obsession leads to destruction	Santiago is physically defeated but retains honor

The next prompt requested ChatGPT to present the information as an infographic:

Figure 2.1 Infographic generated by ChatGPT comparing Moby Dick and The Old Man and the Sea

Takeaways for Chapter 2

This chapter delves into the inner workings of ChatGPT, outlining its five foundational competencies, how it works, and ways it can be used for productivity as well as highly valued "soft skills." It also describes some limitations and cautions.

1. The five core competencies ChatGPT is trained to do are:
    a. Idea expansion
    b. Information structuring

    c. Content transformation
    d. Pattern recognition
    e. Synthesis and summarization
2. Use these five competencies to move beyond viewing ChatGPT as just a text generator. It can help you with workflow, organization, and content. Beyond these productivity benefits, it can enhance highly valued thinking, communicating, learning, and planning skills.
3. ChatGPT's knowledge base is vast, but it is not a database. It is sourced from publicly available information such as books, articles, and newspapers. The original text is not stored. Each response is generated not retrieved.
4. Due to complex training, ChatGPT is extremely flexible. It responds by analyzing prompts and previous conversations, then connecting them to its pretrained knowledge base of patterns.
5. ChatGPT does not understand reality or experience emotions. It can make errors, sound plausible while being wrong, and sound friendly, helpful, and supportive—but it is not human.
6. Responsible use of AI is essential and underpins its value to you. Using AI to bypass genuine learning is unethical and counterproductive. Using judgment is essential when evaluating accuracy.

PART 2

Speed Up Routine Writing

Most professionals spend far too much time on short, routine documents. This section shows you how to speed them up using ChatGPT, without sacrificing clarity, tone, or quality. You'll learn how to draft, edit, and polish emails, reports, announcements, and social posts efficiently.

You'll also learn how to create reusable templates for repetitive writing, freeing you up for more important tasks.

The techniques you learn in these chapters will be useful when you explore deeper and more analytic techniques in Chapters 5 and 6.

CHAPTER 3

Drafting Everyday Communications

Writing is easy. All you have to do is cross out the wrong words.

—Mark Twain

ChatGPT excels at creating routine communications, like emails, announcements, thank-you notes, and other everyday documents. These messages are meant to be clear and professional, but their value usually ends once they're sent. Unlike a policy, proposal, or legal document, they aren't designed for repeated reference. The recipient might reply, or the exchange may become part of an ongoing conversation, but each individual message stands alone.

You may write dozens of these in a day. They often take more time than you'd like, or you might rush and end up with something less polished than you want. ChatGPT is effective at saving you time without compromising the quality of your communications. By giving it a brief prompt with your key points, it will generate a well-structured draft that you only need to tweak before sending. Once you're comfortable with the process, you'll save time and consistently produce professional communications.

ChatGPT also supports templates for recurring documents, like meeting agendas or weekly progress reports. These documents typically follow a set structure but need fresh details each time. With templates, you can produce them faster, ensure accuracy and consistency, and cut down on repetitive effort. For more on creating and using templates, see Chapter 4.

How to Create Routine Documents

Creating routine documents is straightforward. A single, well-thought-out prompt is often all it takes to produce a near-perfect document that only requires a brief review and a few tweaks.

Here is a simple prompt that instructs ChatGPT to generate an email. It's not a great prompt because it doesn't explain why a raise is warranted. Nonetheless, with just a simple prompt, it generated a solid, if generic, e-mail with suggested information for you to supply before the next draft.

Write my boss an email saying I deserve a raise.

ChatGPT:

Subject: Request for Salary Adjustment

Dear [Boss's Name],

I hope this message finds you well. I am writing to discuss the possibility of a salary adjustment to reflect my contributions to the team and the value I bring to [Company Name].

Over the past [timeframe], I have taken on [specific tasks or responsibilities you've excelled in], and I'm proud to have achieved [specific achievements, metrics, or outcomes, e.g., increased revenue, improved processes, led successful projects]. These accomplishments have not only contributed to the team's success but also align with our broader goals at [Company Name].

Additionally, I have [mention any upskilling, certifications, or new responsibilities], which further enhance my ability to perform at a high level and support our objectives.

Given these contributions and the value they bring, I would like to request a salary adjustment to [suggested range or percentage increase, if comfortable]. I am confident that this adjustment reflects my dedication, performance, and the market standards for my role.

I deeply appreciate the opportunities I've had to grow at [Company Name], and I'm excited to continue contributing to our success. I would be happy to meet and discuss this in more detail at your convenience.

Thank you for your time and consideration. I look forward to your thoughts.

Best regards,

[Your Full Name]
[Your Position]

As you can see, ChatGPT produced a strong generic email in response to your vague prompt but left a number of details for you to fill in (everything in [square brackets]). You will get a better result if you provide the key points up front. This allows ChatGPT to integrate them into the email more smoothly.

Creating a More Customized Email

Continuing with the scenario above, to improve your chances of getting a raise, include personal details in your prompt. Here is an example:

> **Write a persuasive email to my boss, Anne, asking for a meeting to discuss my compensation. The style should be professional, direct, and confident. Please highlight my value to the company by including these accomplishments:**
>
> - **Developed a new customer support process that reduced costs by 15% and increased satisfaction.**
> - **Completed management training, adding new insights and skills.**
> - **Ready to use these skills to expand my role and help the company succeed.**

In this prompt, you name the recipient, specify the desired tone, and list specific accomplishments. This detail enables ChatGPT to generate a more personalized and persuasive email.

> *ChatGPT:*
>
> *Dear Anne,*
>
> *I hope you're doing well. I'm reaching out to request a meeting with you to discuss my compensation and the value I bring to the company.*
>
> *Over the past [timeframe], I've worked to contribute meaningfully to our team's success. Specifically, I developed a new customer support process that has reduced costs by 15% while significantly increasing customer satisfaction. Additionally, I recently completed a management training course that has provided me with a fresh perspective and enhanced skills in leadership and strategic thinking.*

I am eager to leverage these new skills to expand my role and deliver even greater results for the company. Given my contributions and my ongoing commitment to our success, I believe it's an appropriate time to discuss my compensation.

Please let me know a convenient time for us to meet. I appreciate your time and consideration and look forward to the opportunity to discuss this further.

Best regards,
[Your Full Name]
[Your Position]

In addition to the list of your accomplishments, the prompt specifies the desired style: "professional, direct, and confident." You can experiment with different styles to find the tone that fits you best. Chapter 14 covers styles and tones in detail.

When you write a prompt to create a routine document, follow these three steps:

1. Be specific about the document's purpose and audience.
2. Clearly indicate the desired tone and style, for example, formal, conversational, concise, and direct.
3. Include key points you want incorporated, by using bullet points or a numbered list.

Create some prompts and experiment to see how ChatGPT responds.

Personalizing Messages

ChatGPT is great for quick, personalized messages, like thank-you notes, invitations, or short social media posts. Try these prompts:

- **Write a friendly thank-you email to a client for their business. Mention it was a real pleasure meeting you yesterday. I hope you enjoy the carpet. I think it will look beautiful in your new home.**
- **Create a LinkedIn post announcing our new team member, Ayesha Patel who is an award-winning designer and will be available to assist our clients with their marketing projects.**

A few minutes dedicated to messages like these go a long way in helping you stay connected with clients and colleagues. It's important to include a personal comment, when possible. People respond better to communications with a personal touch than they do to communications that feel mass-produced.

Bullet Point Input

A useful way to create documents with the content and flow you want is to provide ChatGPT with a list of bullet points and request that they be expanded into full text. This can save you a lot of time by getting you a quick first draft without spending a lot of time on the exact wording. It's easier to edit than create.

Imagine that your organization has implemented a new hybrid policy for remote work, and you need to present it to your team. Here is a prompt that uses bullet points to guide ChatGPT:

Use the bullet points that follow to create a clear, concise, and engaging statement of our new hybrid policy on remote work.

- **We have a new policy on remote work.**
- **All employees are required to be in the office a minimum of three days per week.**
- **You may work remotely for two days weekly, if you desire.**
- **All staff are to be in the office on Wednesdays.**
- **Please inform your manager what days you plan to work remotely.**

ChatGPT:

We're introducing a new hybrid remote work policy. All employees are required to be in the office at least three days a week, with everyone on-site every Wednesday. You may choose to work remotely up to two days per week—just let your manager know which days you prefer.

If you prefer a more formal tone, write: "Please make it more formal."

ChatGPT:

We are implementing a new hybrid remote work policy. All employees are required to be present in the office a minimum of three days per week, with mandatory in-office attendance on Wednesdays. Employees may work remotely up to two days per week, if desired. Please inform your manager of your chosen remote workdays.

You can use the bullet list input as a "brain dump" when you don't have a clear flow. Just create bullet points as you think of them and ask ChatGPT to organize them before generating the document.

Refining the Draft

Sometimes ChatGPT's first response is close, but not exactly what you want. To minimize manual editing, ask ChatGPT for specific changes until the draft is almost right, then make any final tweaks yourself.

If you receive a draft that clearly misses the mark, such as a marketing piece that doesn't resonate, you can ask ChatGPT to "try again." It will generate a new version.

Because ChatGPT remembers the conversation in the same chat session, you can request adjustments without rewriting your entire prompt. Just say what you'd like to change. You can adjust the:

1. Length of the document
2. Reading level
3. Tone, style, and voice
4. Output format
5. Language

We'll demonstrate how to apply the five types of adjustments using another prompt:

Write a paragraph describing what we should do about plastic waste.

Plastic pollution threatens our environment, especially from single-use containers that pile up in landfills and oceans. Recycling alone isn't enough—many plastics aren't actually recycled. We need to choose reusable or biodegradable alternatives, support policies that limit plastic waste, and make conscious daily choices to reduce our plastic footprint.

Following are examples of how ChatGPT responded to each request for an adjustment in how its response is presented.

Adjusting the Length

You can ask ChatGPT to make the text longer or shorter. For example:

Rewrite the paragraph so it is two sentences long.

Chat GPT: Plastic pollution threatens our environment, especially from single-use containers that accumulate in landfills and oceans. To address this, we need to choose reusable or biodegradable alternatives, support policies that limit plastic waste, and make conscious daily choices to reduce our plastic footprint.

Increase the length to 75 words.

ChatGPT: Plastic pollution poses a serious threat to our environment, especially from single-use containers that accumulate in landfills and oceans, harming wildlife and natural ecosystems. Unfortunately, recycling alone isn't enough to solve the problem, since many plastics are never actually recycled. To make a meaningful difference, we should opt for reusable or biodegradable alternatives whenever possible, support policies aimed at reducing plastic waste, and make conscious choices each day to lower our plastic footprint and protect our planet for future generations.

Adjusting Reading Level

You can ask ChatGPT to adjust the generated text to fit the reading level of your audience.

Change the reading level to make it appropriate for a 10 year old child.

ChatGPT: Plastic pollution is hurting our planet, especially when we use things like plastic bottles or bags just once and then throw them away. Recycling helps, but it's not enough. We can all help by using things that can be reused or will break down safely, and by making smart choices every day to use less plastic.

Change the reading level to make it appropriate for a Ph.D. scientist.

ChatGPT: Plastic pollution presents a significant environmental challenge, with single-use containers contributing substantially to anthropogenic waste streams and the accumulation of persistent polymers in terrestrial and marine ecosystems. Despite widespread recycling initiatives, the efficacy remains limited due to contamination, downcycling, and infrastructural shortcomings. Addressing this issue requires a systemic shift toward reusable or biodegradable alternatives, robust policy interventions to restrict plastic production and waste, and sustained individual and collective behavioral change to mitigate the long-term ecological and public health impacts of plastic proliferation.

Adjusting Tone, Style, and Voice

Tone and style are important concepts in writing, especially for business communication. *Tone* refers to the emotional attitude or mood conveyed in your writing, such as friendly, formal, confident, or urgent. *Style* is the way you express your ideas: structure, word choice, and sentence complexity. For example, your style might be concise and direct, or it could be detailed and descriptive.

While there is a technical distinction between tone and style, you don't need to stress about it. You can use different combinations of tone and style to suit your document. What matters is that you choose the approach that best fits your audience and your message.

Together, your tone and style create your *voice*: the overall personality or "feel" of your writing. Voice may also be part of your brand. In Chapter

14, we'll explore tone, style, and voice in more detail. For now, here are useful combinations you can try for routine business documents:

- Friendly and conversational—Good for emails and team updates.
- Formal and concise—Best for official announcements or policies.
- Confident and direct—Effective in proposals or performance reviews.
- Respectful and detailed—Useful for customer communications or feedback.
- Upbeat and clear—Great for invitations or thank-you notes.

Experiment with these combinations to see the impact on the message.

Friendly and Conversational

ChatGPT: Plastic pollution is a big problem, especially with all those single-use containers piling up everywhere. While recycling is helpful, it just isn't enough. If we all try to use reusable or biodegradable things and make small changes every day, we can really make a difference together. Let's help our planet!

Formal and Concise

ChatGPT: Plastic pollution poses a significant environmental threat, particularly from single-use containers. Recycling efforts are insufficient, as many plastics are not processed. Adopting reusable or biodegradable alternatives and supporting waste-reducing policies are essential steps for minimizing our collective plastic footprint.

Confident and Direct

ChatGPT: Plastic pollution is damaging our environment, and single-use containers are a major cause. Recycling alone won't solve this. We must switch to reusable or biodegradable options, push for stronger policies, and make daily choices that cut plastic waste for good.

Respectful and Detailed

> *ChatGPT: We recognize that plastic pollution is a growing concern, with single-use containers playing a major role in environmental damage. While recycling has its merits, it often falls short. By choosing reusable or biodegradable alternatives, supporting effective policies, and making mindful choices every day, we can work together to protect our environment.*

Upbeat and Clear

> *ChatGPT: There's good news—even small actions can help fight plastic pollution! Single-use containers are a challenge, but by picking reusable or biodegradable products and supporting smart policies, we can all make a positive impact. Every step you take helps create a cleaner, healthier planet for everyone.*

Formatting Output

You can specify output format in the original prompt or ask for a different format once the text has been generated. We'll look at a few common output formats here based on the prompt:

> **Give me a list of useful output formats I can request.**

To request a different output format, after the original document has been generated, simply say:

> **Now format it as [format type]**

The following is a short list of various formats ChatGPT could use to present the same information about plastic waste:

- Bullet points
- Numbered list
- Table

- Checklist
- Q&A Format

The following illustrate each of these formats using the prompt template.

Bullet Points

Now format it as bullet points.

Following is the output in bullet format.

- *Plastic pollution is a major environmental threat.*
- *Single-use plastic containers contribute heavily to the problem.*
- *Recycling isn't enough—many plastics aren't recycled.*
- *Alternatives include reusable or biodegradable containers.*
- *People can help by making conscious choices and supporting policies that reduce plastic waste.*

Numbered List

Now format it as a numbered list.

Here is the output in a numbered list:

1. *Plastic pollution endangers the environment.*
2. *Single-use containers are a significant source of waste.*
3. *Recycling systems have limitations; much plastic isn't recycled.*
4. *Reusable and biodegradable options are available.*
5. *Individuals can help by reducing use and supporting better policies.*

Table

Now format it in a table.

Following is the output in a table:

Table 3.1 ChatGPT's presentation in table format rather than text

Issue	Details/actions
Plastic pollution	Environmental threat from plastic waste
Single-use plastics	Major contributor to landfills and oceans
Recycling problems	Not all plastics get recycled
Alternatives	Reusable and biodegradable containers
What you can do	Choose alternatives, support policies, make conscious choices

Checklist

Now format it as a checklist.

This is the output as a numbered list:

1. Avoid single-use plastic containers
2. Choose reusable or biodegradable alternatives
3. Understand the limitations of recycling
4. Support policies to reduce plastic waste
5. Make daily conscious choices to reduce your plastic use

Q&A Format

Now format it in a Q&A format.

This is the output in Question & Answer format:

Q: Why is plastic pollution a problem?
A: It harms the environment, especially from single-use containers.
Q: Is recycling enough to solve it?
A: No, many plastics aren't recycled.
Q: What are the alternatives?
A: Use reusable or biodegradable containers.
Q: How can people help?
A: Make smarter choices and support policies limiting plastic waste.

Executive Summary

An *executive summary* is different from a format. It is typically used in the front of longer documents which selects and presents a new, short version that captures relevant information or conclusions contained in a lengthier report.

The following prompt requests an executive summary about the plastic pollution problem. Notice that are still in the same chat session, so ChatGPT remembers the conversation.

Provide a concise *executive summary*

Here is the *executive summary* produced based on this prompt:

Plastic pollution, especially from single-use containers, poses a serious environmental risk. Recycling alone isn't sufficient, as much plastic isn't actually recycled. Using reusable or biodegradable alternatives and supporting strong waste-reduction policies are practical steps people can take to reduce plastic pollution.

Step-by-Step Instructions

Instructions are not an *executive summary* or a simple format change. The following prompt will generate a simple list of sequential tasks culled from or in addition to the original text response.

List step-by-step instructions for implementation

This is the output resulting from this prompt:

1. Recognize the dangers of plastic pollution and single-use containers.
2. Learn about the limitations of recycling plastic.
3. Switch to reusable or biodegradable containers.
4. Support policies that address plastic waste.
5. Make conscious choices every day to reduce your plastic footprint.

Outline

An outline contains highlights of the content presented in response to the prompt for an explanation of plastic pollution, which may be used to introduce the document generated by ChatGPT.

A sample prompt may be:

Give me a brief outline I can use when presenting my report.

Here is the resulting outline based on the prompt:

- Introduction: Plastic pollution as an environmental threat
- The danger of single-use plastic containers
- Problems with recycling plastic
- Suggested alternatives: reusable and biodegradable options
- What individuals can do to make a difference

Social Media Post (LinkedIn Example)

A social media post is a brief, public statement of an opinion, policy decision, promotion or other information. This requires a specific format, tone, suggested tags or other short communication.

Here is a sample prompt:

Please draft a post I can use on our LinkedIn site about our position on plastics pollution and suggest hashtags that would generate comments, clicks or sharing.

Here is the resulting output:

Plastic pollution is a growing threat—especially from single-use containers. Recycling isn't enough; many plastics end up in landfills. Let's choose reusable or biodegradable alternatives and support policies that cut plastic waste. Every daily choice counts! #Sustainability #ReducePlastic

Case Study or Scenario

ChatGPT can also be useful to provide a case study for training or a scenario to introduce a topic. It is usually written in a short story format for illustrative purposes and generate discussion or reaction. To be most effective, it needs to sound realistic to the audience.

Here is a sample prompt:

Please draft a case study I can use to create as part of a program to build awareness among our staff

Here is the resulting output to this prompt:

Maria noticed her office was using hundreds of single-use plastic containers each week. She introduced reusable lunchboxes and educated her colleagues about the limits of recycling. Over time, plastic waste dropped sharply, and the office adopted a policy to support biodegradable alternatives—demonstrating the real impact of individual and collective action.

Language and Translation

Changing language is easy. Just ask ChatGPT to produce or translate the text into whatever languages you want. Here is a sample prompt:

Translate the paragraph into French, Spanish, and Chinese.

Following is the output, translated into French, Spanish and Chinese (Simplified):

French
La pollution plastique menace notre environnement, en particulier à cause des contenants à usage unique qui s'accumulent dans les décharges et les océans. Le recyclage seul ne suffit pas, car de nombreux plastiques ne sont pas réellement recyclés. Nous devons choisir des alternatives réutilisables ou biodégradables, soutenir des politiques qui limitent les déchets plastiques et faire des choix quotidiens conscients pour réduire notre empreinte plastique.

Spanish
La contaminación por plásticos amenaza nuestro medio ambiente, especialmente por los envases de un solo uso que se acumulan en vertederos y océanos. Reciclar no es suficiente, ya que muchos plásticos no se reciclan realmente. Debemos elegir alternativas reutilizables o biodegradables, apoyar políticas que limiten los residuos plásticos y tomar decisiones diarias conscientes para reducir nuestra huella de plástico.

Chinese (Simplified)
塑料污染威胁着我们的环境，尤其是那些堆积在垃圾填埋场和海洋中的一次性容器。仅靠回收是远远不够的，因为许多塑料实际上并没有被回收。我们需要选择可重复使用或可生物降解的替代品，支持限制塑料垃圾的政策，并在日常生活中有意识地减少我们的塑料足迹。

If you are curious, yes, these translations were verified for accuracy and (using a screen reader) for pronunciation and authenticity of accent!

Try It Out

Experiment with drafting documents using the suggestions below. Once you have a draft, try out different formats and style/tone combinations.

- Write an email inviting staff to a summer picnic.
  Ask them to bring their familie. Use bullet points to describe the food and activities. Write the initial draft in a straightforward tone. Then ask ChatGPT to try again to make it more persuasive and engaging.
- Create an announcement for a lost kitten.
  Ask anyone who has seen the kitten to contact you. Once you have a draft, ask ChatGPT to add additional details.
- Write a thank-you note to your customer, Juliette Frances, thanking her for her recent order of a stuffed unicorn toy. Have ChatGPT try different tones: formal, friendly, and motivating.

- Ask for five characteristics of effective team collaboration. Then, request the information as a 60-word essay, a bullet-point list, and a table.
- Ask ChatGPT to write a 60-word essay on actions people can take to help slow down climate change. Then ask ChatGPT to shorten it to 40 words.

Takeaways for Chapter 3

This chapter demonstrates how ChatGPT can help you create routine business communications, from e-mails and announcements to thank-you notes and recurring documents like meeting agendas. The chapter walks you through building prompts, adding key details, and refining drafts by asking ChatGPT for changes in tone, style, length, or format. You'll also see how to use bullet points to guide document creation, experiment with different writing styles, and request translations or alternative formats.

1. ChatGPT streamlines routine communications—including emails, announcements, and thank-you notes—saving you time and improving professionalism.
2. Clear, specific prompts with key details lead to stronger, more personalized drafts.
3. Refine drafts: You can easily adjust length, reading level, tone, style, language, and format by requesting changes.
4. Bullet points are effective ways to specify content and flow when creating drafts.
5. Multiple output formats: you can request various output formats such as bullet lists, tables, checklists, executive summaries, or Q&A.
6. Experimenting with tone and style helps you find the right voice for each situation.
7. Translations are quick and easy, making it simple to reach a wider audience.

CHAPTER 4

Document Templates

A good template forces good thinking.
—Chip Heath and Dan Heath, Made to Stick (2007)

If you often write documents where the structure stays the same but the details change, templates can save you significant time and effort. A template provides a reusable framework for documents like meeting agendas, status updates, blog and social media posts, and routine customer communications.

Fixed Templates

Imagine you own a pet store and want to send a thank-you note to each customer who makes a purchase. You do this every day. To create this simple template, provide ChatGPT with:

1. A prompt instructing ChatGPT to write the email.
2. The template itself.
3. The specific details to insert.

Here's a complete prompt for a reusable template, followed by the specific details for this customer email:

Please create an email using the following template and details.

Template:
Subject: Thank you for your order!
Dear [customer name],
Thank you for your order! We appreciate your purchase of [item description].
Sincerely,
The Puppy Palace Sales Team

Details:
customer name: Bill
item description: Bark-O-Matic Dog Toy

Both the template and the details are clearly labeled. This helps ChatGPT understand exactly what to do. Each detail is identified so ChatGPT knows which field to fill in (e.g., "customer name: Bill"). Here is the output generated:

ChatGPT:
Subject: Thank you for your order!
Dear Bill,
Thank you for your order! We appreciate your purchase of Bark-O-Matic Dog Toy.
Sincerely,
The Puppy Palace Sales Team

Creating Multiple Documents Using a Fixed Template

If business is good, you may have to produce many emails at the end of the day. You can do them all with a single prompt and a stack of details:

Please create an email for each recipient using the following template and sets of details.

Template:
Subject: Thank you for your order!
Dear [customer name],
Thank you for your order! We appreciate your purchase of [item description].
Sincerely,
The Puppy Palace Sales Team

Details:
customer name: Bill
item description: Bark-O-Matic Dog Toy
customer name: Janet

item description: Purrfect Cat Tower
customer name: Steven
item description: Hamster Habitat Deluxe
customer name: Mary
item description: Aquarium Starter Kit

This will generate all the emails at once. The pet store templates above are *fixed templates*. Every document they create has exactly the same structure.

Flexible Templates

Flexible templates adapt their output based on the details you provide. They can automatically add, remove, or rephrase sections based on your input, so you can create documents with parts that change week to week or appear only when needed. We'll cover three flexible template features:

- *Repetitive* sections for lists with any number of items.
- *Conditional* sections that appear only when you provide matching details.
- *Default values* that remain unless you replace them.

These options are explained further in the sections that follow.

Repetitive Sections

Imagine you're creating a weekly report that lists the status of each project your team is working on. The number of projects may change from week to week. To handle this, include a repetitive section in your template:

[For each project:]
Project: [project name]
Status: [status]
Notes: [notes]

The lines under [For each project:] (project name, status, and notes) will be repeated for every project in your detail list. To make the list easier to read, you can ask ChatGPT to insert a separator between project summaries. This could be a dashed line, a blank line, bullet points, numbers, or another symbol. Here is the prompt, template, and details:

> **Please generate a weekly project summary using the template and project details below.**
>
> **For each project, insert the project information and add a dashed line (---) after each project summary except the last one.**
>
> **TEMPLATE:**
> **Weekly Project Summary – [Date]**
>
> **[For each project:]**
> **Project: [project name]**
> **Status: [status]**
> **Notes: [notes]**
>
> **PROJECT DETAILS:**
> **Date: May 27**
>
> **project name: Website Redesign**
> **status: On Track**
> **notes: All design mockups approved.**
>
> **project name: Mobile App Launch**
> **status: Delayed**
> **notes: Waiting on final QA testing.**
>
> **project name: Marketing Campaign**
> **status: Completed**
> **notes: Campaign wrapped with 10% above target.**

This will produce the output:

Weekly Project Summary – May 27
Project: Website Redesign
Status: On Track
Notes: All design mockups approved.

Project: Mobile App Launch

Status: Delayed
Notes: Waiting on final QA testing.

Project: Marketing Campaign
Status: Completed
Notes: Campaign wrapped with 10% above target.

Since ChatGPT uses natural language, you don't have to use the exact words shown in the examples. Just make sure you are *clear* about what you want and *consistent* with your labeling. You can adapt the repeating section to fit any kind of list, as long as you keep the *names* and *fields* consistent everywhere they appear. For clarity:

- Match labels in your template and details item.
- Group details together and separate them with a blank line.
- Add a separator (blank or dashed line) between repeated sections for readability.

Conditional Sections

Use a conditional section to include content only when there are *details* to show. This prevents headings from appearing above empty sections. Here is an example of generating a newsletter that may have different sections from week to week:

Use this flexible template to generate a newsletter. If any sections are missing, reword the output so it reads naturally.

TEMPLATE:
Newsletter – [Date]

Announcements:
[Optional—display only if announcements are in the detail list]

New Staff:
[Optional—display only if new staff are in the detail list]

Employee Events:

[Optional—display only if employee events are in the detail list]

DETAILS:

Announcements: There will be a fire drill on Thursday.

Employee Events: Picnic is this weekend. Bring your family.

When ChatGPT generates the newsletter, it will omit the "New Staff" section since there are no details for it. This approach ensures your documents stay complete and professional, even when some details are missing.

Default Values

A default value is text ChatGPT uses when you don't provide your own. Write it in square brackets so ChatGPT knows to replace it if details are given.

Here is an example of a newsletter template with default text at the end that can be replaced with a detail when desired.

[Default Close: We are observing summer hours until September 1.]

If "Close" details are provided, ChatGPT will use them. Otherwise, it will use the default text. The label ("Default Close:") will not appear in the final document.

Use the template and details below to create the newsletter.

Show a section only if there are matching details.

If a section contains a default value (in the format [Default Close: ...]), replace it if "Close" details are given, or use the default if none are provided.

Do not include the words "Default Close:" in the output—only the text after it.

TEMPLATE:

Newsletter – [Date]

Announcements:

[Optional—display only if announcements are in the detail list]

Employee Events:

[Optional—display only if employee events are in the detail list]

[Default Close: We are observing summer hours until September 1.

DETAILS:

Announcements: The annual meeting is scheduled for Thursday.

When ChatGPT runs this, it will:

- Show Announcements with the meeting detail.
- Skip Employee Events because no detail is provided.
- Include the Default Close because no "Close" detail is provided.

Saving Templates

ChatGPT has no built-in template library. While some versions offer persistent memory, it stores only facts and preferences, not full documents or templates. The most reliable approach is to save templates in a tool like Word, Notion, or Evernote and paste them into ChatGPT when needed. In some versions you can also connect to One Drive or Google Drive.

Within a single chat session, you can ask ChatGPT to remember a template and assign it a name using a prompt like:

- **Please remember the following template as [Template Name]. I will refer to it by this name in future prompts during this session.**
- **[Paste your template here]**
- **Please confirm when you have saved it.**

After doing this, you can refer to the template by name for the rest of that session. When you start a new chat, you will need to reintroduce the template.

Building Templates Interactively

Here we introduce *Guided Q&A*, which is a powerful interactive technique in which ChatGPT asks you questions and alters the dialog based on your responses. Building proficiency with this technique is one of the most effective ways to interact with ChatGPT. You'll find other applications for this technique in Chapters 5 and 6.

It's especially useful if you don't have all the details figured out before you start writing a template. In this example, we will use structured questions to create a template for a monthly team meeting.

I want to create a template for a monthly staff meeting and use it for the next meeting. Can you walk me through the process by asking one question at a time?

ChatGPT:

Great—let's walk through this step by step. I'll help you build a useful, flexible template you can reuse easily.

Step 1: What's the general purpose of your monthly staff meetings?

(For example: project updates, team alignment, planning, morale, issue resolution?)

You:

I want to share announcements that everyone should know about, find out any projects that may be at risk and need extra support, and align the team around priorities for the coming month when we will do this again.

ChatGPT:

Excellent—that gives us a clear purpose: communication, risk awareness, and alignment.

Step 2: Do these meetings usually follow a predictable structure or flow?

For example, do you typically start with announcements, then go around the team, then wrap up with priorities—or is it more free-form?

You:

We do it exactly as you suggest. I try to maintain the same flow each month so the team has a sense of how to prepare.

ChatGPT:

Perfect—that consistency makes it ideal for a fixed-structure, flexible-content template.

Step 3: Do you typically prepare the agenda yourself, or do team members contribute items in advance?

(And do you want space in the template to include any pre-submitted items or topics?)

You:

I do it myself. I send out the agenda several days before the meeting and if anyone has a topic they want included they can reach out to me.

ChatGPT:

Great—that means the agenda is primarily authored by you, with optional input from others. We'll include a placeholder for optional team-submitted topics, but it won't be required.

Step 4: How do you send the agenda—email, calendar invite, shared doc?

(And would you like ChatGPT to generate the full message or just the agenda section?)

You:

Just generate the agenda. I will send it as an email attachment with a calendar invite.

ChatGPT:

Got it—so the goal is to generate a standalone agenda document you can attach. We'll focus on clean structure, clear sections, and optional flexibility.

Step 5: What standard sections should appear in every meeting agenda?

Here's a suggested list based on your earlier goals—feel free to confirm or edit:

Announcements

Project Risk Check-In

Upcoming Priorities

Team-Submitted Topics (optional)

Wrap-Up & Next Steps

Would you like to use these, or make any changes or additions?

You:

I would like number 4 to be an open discussion of topics that team members are concerned about.

ChatGPT:

Perfect—we'll revise item 4 to reflect an open discussion section where team members can raise concerns or issues in the moment.

Here's the updated structure:

Announcements

Project Risk Check-In

Upcoming Priorities

Open Discussion – Team Concerns or Topics
Wrap-Up & Next Steps

Step 6: Do you want to include date, time, and meeting location (or Zoom link) at the top of the agenda each time?
If so, should we include those as placeholders in the template?

You:
Just include the date. We always meet at the same time and if we have remote attendees I will place the Zoom link in the invite.

ChatGPT:
Understood—we'll include a [Date] placeholder at the top, but skip time and location.
Step 7: Would you like each agenda item to include optional notes or prompts beneath them (e.g., "List any key announcements here" or "Be ready to flag any projects that need help")—or do you prefer a clean list of headings only?

You:
I think an optional notes area at the end would be useful. If I have nothing special I will leave it out. But if there is a special issue I want to communicate we can use that space.

ChatGPT:
Excellent—that gives us a clean structure with a flexible notes section at the end, included only when needed.
We're ready to build the template. Would you like it displayed with square brackets for placeholders (e.g., [Date]) and formatted as a ready-to-copy template?

You:
Yes.
ChatGPT:
Here is your Monthly Staff Meeting Agenda Template, formatted with square brackets for easy reuse and customization:
Monthly Staff Meeting Agenda
Date: [Date]

Announcements
[List any key updates or company-wide news.]

Project Risk Check-In
[Be ready to identify any projects that may be delayed, blocked, or need additional support.]

Upcoming Priorities
[Outline the team's focus areas for the coming month.]

Open Discussion – Team Concerns or Topics
[An open forum for team members to raise issues, ask questions, or share suggestions.]

Wrap-Up & Next Steps
[Summarize action items or agreements from the meeting.]

Optional Notes:
[Use this space for special messages, reminders, or highlights that don't fit elsewhere.]

They use natural language, so you don't have to follow restrictive syntax. You can design them in any text editor or have ChatGPT help by asking structured questions and building the template from your answers.

How Nora Got Her Friday Back

Nora dreaded her Friday status reports. Each week was different, and writing it took her at least an hour. Fortunately, Nora read this chapter! The third time she missed her train, she prompted ChatGPT:

Can you help me create a reusable weekly report format that's easy to update, even when content varies?

Responding to its structured questions, she created a template with sections for project updates, next steps, blockers, and notes. The first time she used it, she completed her report in 30 minutes. The second time in 10.

Nora's manager is happy with the consistent, on-time reports, and Nora is happy because she no longer misses her train on Fridays.

Takeaways for Chapter 4

Templates are helpful when you need to create recurring documents with the same structure but different details. For example, you might use a template for project status reports, where the format stays the same, but the details change for each project.

Templates can be fixed or flexible. Fixed templates produce one or multiple documents with the same structure

Flexible templates allow you to create documents with repeating sections, conditional sections and default text for missing data details you provide. They can automatically add, remove, or rephrase sections based on your prompt, so you can create documents with parts that change.

1. Templates save time and effort by providing a reusable structure for repeatable documents.
2. Fixed templates are used when only a few details, such as names, dates, or topics, change each time.
3. Flexible templates allow sections to be skipped or reworded when certain data are missing.
4. Templates can be created interactively by having ChatGPT ask you questions and assemble the template based on your responses.
5. Use placeholders like [Date] or [Customer Name] to indicate where input should be placed.
6. The most reliable way to save templates is as text files in a notes app or word processor, so you can easily copy and paste them into ChatGPT as needed.

PART 3

Techniques You Can Build On

In this part, we move to deeper uses of ChatGPT as we cover practical techniques that move you beyond surface tasks, using ChatGPT to explore ideas, uncover insight, and work with greater depth. AI can help you think more clearly, plan with greater precision, and expand your skills, knowledge, and resilience in ways that change how you approach challenges.

You can adapt and expand these techniques to fit your needs and style. Each stands alone: choose the ones that help you now, and return as your scope, responsibilities, and goals evolve.

This part contains five chapters.

Chapter 5 focuses on boosting productivity: asking better questions, handling information overload, managing meetings, and communicating in ways that engage and influence. Be sure to read the first section that describes Guided Q&A – a powerful technique for initiating dialogs with ChatGPT that is the foundation of many techniques.

Chapter 6 covers interactive conversations that use Guided Q&A to help you clarify ideas, turn ideas into plans, prepare arguments, and deal with situations where your audience has different, and potentially clashing, perspectives, and rehearse difficult conversations.

Chapter 7 covers techniques that help you with project management.

Chapter 8 covers strategy research and planning.

Chapter 9 presents ways to use ChatGPT as a teacher to grow your expertise and skills.

As your work and career progress, return to these techniques to help you think more clearly, act more decisively, and find solutions others may miss.

CHAPTER 5

Streamline Everyday Tasks

Efficiency is doing things right; effectiveness is doing the right things.

—Peter Drucker

This chapter focuses on boosting productivity. Writing, outlining, editing, research, reading long documents, planning meetings, and organizing notes are necessary parts of knowledge work that can eat up time and energy. The techniques in this chapter can lead to big gains. Techniques in this chapter:

- Two powerful ways to work with ChatGPT
- How to phrase a question
- Ask ChatGPT how it can help
- Build a document interactively
- Edit and improve your writing
- Beat writer's block
- Make your writing more persuasive
- Plan and run better meetings
- Use ChatGPT to work with data
- Use Agents in ChatGPT
- Summarize long documents
- Build a custom GPT

Two Powerful Ways to Work With ChatGPT

Choose the interaction style that works for you.

We describe two interaction styles you can use with ChatGPT. Both appeared in earlier chapters; here, we look at them in more depth. The two styles: *Ask & Refine*, and *Guided Q&A*, can be used on their own or combined in a single chat.

Most people use ChatGPT the same way they use a search engine. They ask quick questions and expect quick answers. That approach works well for simple facts or small tasks, but it barely scratches the surface of what ChatGPT can do.

ChatGPT is not just a search tool. It can help you plan, think, create, and solve problems. But the best outcome is when AI enhances human capacity to apply experience, judgment, knowledge of the environment you're working in and emotions. By using these interaction patterns, you can use ChatGPT in a more powerful way.

The main difference between the two styles is whether *you* or the AI takes the lead:

- In Ask & Refine, *you* take the lead by asking questions or giving prompts. ChatGPT responds. You refine the result through follow-up prompts.
- In Guided Q&A, *ChatGPT* takes the lead by asking you questions to clarify your needs. It then builds a focused response based on your answers.

These two approaches form the foundation for every technique in this book. Let's look at them in more detail.

Ask & Refine

The Ask & Refine style is the simplest way to work with ChatGPT. You give a prompt, ChatGPT responds, and you refine the answer by asking follow-up questions or requesting changes. This process is often called *iterative refinement* and works best when you already know what you want and can describe it clearly. Examples of Ask & Refine include:

- Asking ChatGPT for specific information.
- Editing text to make it clearer.

- Rewriting an email to sound more professional or persuasive.
- Creating a short list of ideas or next steps.

This style can be used at different levels of detail. Sometimes you may ask a simple, open question like, "What are three ways to improve a team meeting?" Other times, you might provide more detail to help ChatGPT focus, such as "I manage a team of eight engineers. Our meetings run too long and feel unfocused. Suggest three ways to improve our team meetings." Generally, the more detail you provide, the better the response.

Ask & Refine also builds on ideas you've already seen in Chapter 3, where we discuss iterative refinement in terms of follow-up prompts, changes in style, tone, length, output format, and target audience.

Guided Q&A

The Guided Q&A style flips the process. Instead of answering right away, ChatGPT asks you questions to gather the information it needs. This style is especially useful when your goals are not fully clear, when the topic is new to you, or when the task is complex and open-ended.Answering the questions *one at a time*, you break the problem into smaller pieces and slow down to consider if you're asking the best question rather than assuming that you do. This technique helps develop build better analytical and critical thinking skills that are the foundation of agile thinking. Examples of Guided Q&A applications include:

- Planning a product launch.
- Drafting an article or presentation.
- Preparing for a job interview or difficult conversation.
- Proposing a new process or policy.

By asking structured questions, ChatGPT helps you clarify what you want, uncover gaps in your thinking, and build a better result. This approach is often faster and more effective for complex work than starting with a single, unrefined prompt.

Table 5.1 How best to use Interaction Styles

Style	How it works	Best for
Ask & Refine	You give a prompt. ChatGPT responds. You refine your result through follow-up prompts.	Situations where you know exactly what you want. You can use prompts to validate or expand on the response or ask for alternatives that occur to you based on the initial response.
Guided Q&A	ChatGPT asks questions, then you respond.	Your ideas or what information you need are not fully formed; complex or open-ended tasks where some information may not be known at the start or change (e.g., planning); rehearsing conversations or approaches that can help you consider alternative perspectives.

The Importance of Context

With both Ask & Refine and Guided Q&A, you will get the best results if you provide ChatGPT with *context.*

ChatGPT has access to a vast range of information, but it does not know what matters to you. Without guidance, it may produce responses that are correct but unfocused, too general, or unrealistic for your environment.

Context is the detail you add to your prompts that tells ChatGPT where to focus. Without context, ChatGPT has no way to judge what is important or relevant. There are many types of details that you can supply. None are required, but the more detail you share with ChatGPT, the more focused and relevant it will be. Examples of context you can include are:

- Your role (e.g., "I'm a training director or a small tech company.")
- Your task (e.g., "I'm developing a training proposal for the next year.")
- Describing the situation you are addressing (e.g., "There is concern about the cost of training.")
- Your goal (e.g., "I want it to be persuasive and demonstrate cost effectiveness.")
- Your audience and tone (e.g., "I am writing for the senior management.")

- Your preferred format (e.g., "Give me a slide outline.")
- Your environment or culture (e.g., "Avoid jargon—my team prefers plain language.")

You can provide context at any level of detail that makes sense to you:

- Simple: "Tell me the basics of blockchain for a meeting."
- Detailed: "I work in IT. We're exploring blockchain for internal systems. What should I know to guide the discussion?"

When you are working on large projects, you can create a context file to provide ChatGPT with a clear, continuous focus. Context files are discussed in Chapter 10.

Switching Styles as You Work

You can switch between Ask & Refine and Guided Q&A at any point in a chat.

An example of how to switch from Ask & Refine to Guided Q&A:

Prompt: Tell me about climate change.

ChatGPT responds. You aren't satisfied with the response.

Prompt: Help me refine this result. Ask me questions before responding.

By having ChatGPT ask you questions one at a time, you will gain the clarity and context you need to get a more useful response.Here is an example of how to use a prompt to switch from Guided Q&A to direct output:

Can you ask me some questions about climate change to narrow the focus?

ChatGPT begins asking you questions. You are not satisfied with the response.

Here are two sample prompts you could try.

- **Respond to each question ChatGPT asks.**
- **Actually, never mind the questions. Just write a summary that focuses on solutions, not causes.**

When you use a Guided Q&A format, ChatGPT may ask all the questions at once—especially if your prompt is open-ended. You can respond to them together if that suits you. Often, though, it's more effective to have ChatGPT ask you questions one at a time. It will adjust subsequent questions based on your answers, which can help also clarify your thinking as you work through the topic.

To get questions individually, include a line like this in your prompt:

Ask me questions one at a time. Wait to respond until you have enough information.

By adding that instruction, you can turn almost any prompt into a Guided Q&A.

In the techniques that follow, we will use either Ask & Refine or Guided Q&A. However, you can alter the interaction if you want.

How to Phrase a Question

Tap into massive knowledge, presented in the way you want.

Responding to questions is ChatGPT's most basic capability. Researchers have found that the quality of its answer depends heavily on the quality of the prompt. As with most aspects of ChatGPT, there are no hard-and-fast rules. That said, the clearer and more specific your prompt, the better the quality of the response. Here is a short, well-structured prompt:

Summarize the key differences between waterfall and agile project management for non-technical business professionals. Use simple language and present your answer as a bulleted list.

This simple but specific prompt gives ChatGPT a clear task, a defined topic, the audience, and the desired output format.

A good basic skeleton for a simple question prompt is:

Give me [type of response] about [topic or question], intended for [audience or purpose]. Show the results as [output format].

Here is a summary of common prompt elements you can use and where they can be most useful.

Table 5.2 Prompt elements, their purpose and an example

Prompt element	Purpose and example
Give me [type of response]	Clarifies what you want: list, summary, explanation, action plan, step-by-step instructions, or another type of response.
About [topic or question]	Defines the subject you want help with.
Intended for [audience/purpose]	Helps tailor the tone, complexity, and relevance.
Use a tone that is [appropriate to audience/purpose/type]. (Helpful but optional.)	Sets the mood: professional, conversational, persuasive, or others.
Keep it [length]. (Helpful but optional.)	Try short, medium, long or specify number of words or bullet points.
Format [one or more options to consider best way of presentation]. (Helpful but optional.)	Choose bulleted list, numbered list, paragraph, table, chart, Q&A, comparison of pro's-con's, etc.
Focus [emphasis most effective to audience/purpose]. (Helpful but optional.)	Emphasizes what to include, exclude or changes to save editing later.
Constraints [limitations or existing policies]. (Helpful but optional.)	A constraint is a specific guideline, such as word count, time frame, scope, resources available, competing priorities, etc. • Keep it to 100 words. • In 19th-century Europe. • We are on a tight schedule with limited resources. • Only include free tools.
Angle [positioning]. (Helpful but optional.)	Focus on a specific perspective or approach. • Focus on the customer's perspective. • Identify possible objections and ways to respond.

(*Continued*)

Table 5.2 Prompt elements, their purpose and an example (Continued)

Prompt element	Purpose and example
Role play [differences in perspectives] (Helpful but optional)	Ask ChatGPT to respond as if it were a specific role: • Respond as if you were a corporate executive. • Respond as if you were a 14-year old child. • Respond as if you were an angry customer. • Respond as if you weren't understanding me.

As is typical of ChatGPT interactions, you do not have to use these precise words as long as your intent is clear and the prompts are unambiguous.

Ask ChatGPT How It Can Help You

Facing a New Challenge? Ask ChatGPT how it can help.

When you encounter a new or unfamiliar challenge—like a new role, a complex project, a struggle to influence decisions, or you need to quickly understand a technology you've never used before, ask ChatGPT how it can help. It will suggest specific ways it can support you, identify areas you hadn't considered, and offer example prompts to get you started.

Use the template below to explore how ChatGPT can assist with a professional challenge you're facing:

I'm dealing with [briefly describe your challenge, project, or situation].

Here's more context: [explain what you're trying to achieve, what's difficult, or what you're unsure about].

Please suggest specific ways you could help, organized into these categories:

- **Planning and organization**
- **Learning and research**
- **Communication and writing**
- **Decision-making and strategy**
- **Brainstorming and creative thinking**

For each category, include an example prompt I could use to get started.

Example:

I am the newly-hired marketing director of a 45-person software company. The company has a great product but little experience in marketing and sales. I want to hit the ground running with quick wins and lay the foundation for long-term success. How can you help me?

In this example, the prompt did not specify categories for opening the response, so ChatGPT chose the categories itself.

ChatGPT said:

Thanks for the context! Based on your new role and goals, here are specific ways I can help—organized by category:

Planning and Organization

- **Help me outline a 90-day marketing plan with quick wins and long-term priorities.**
- **What marketing metrics should I track in my first quarter?**

Learning and Research

Prompt:

- **Explain the key differences between B2B SaaS marketing and traditional product marketing.**
- **What are common marketing pitfalls for early-stage software companies?**

Communication and Writing

Prompt:

- **Draft a welcome message introducing me to the company as the new marketing director.**

- **Write a one-page product overview for prospects who are unfamiliar with our software.**

Decision-Making and Strategy

Prompt:

- **What low-cost marketing strategies can generate qualified leads quickly?**
- **Help me prioritize between content marketing, paid ads, and partnerships.**

Brainstorming and Creative Thinking

Prompt:

- **Give me five creative campaign ideas to increase brand awareness in our target industry.**
- **What would be a bold but smart move I could take in my first 60 days?**

Let me know which area you'd like to dive into, or if you want help turning any of these into action steps.

Try It Out

Try using a prompt that includes your specific role and industry. Once you get the initial response, follow up on anything that seems useful, ask for more detail, or ask it to try again. It will often give you several options to choose from, for example, regarding tone or what you want to emphasize.

Don't stop at the first answer; dig deeper for details such as alternatives, campaigns that flopped, ROI figures that might be available, and clear actions. You can ask ChatGPT to walk you through any task or process with step-by-step instructions tailored to your situation.

As you go through this process, you'll find that your thinking may have changed based on the information you get back. ChatGPT will go back to the beginning and offer alternatives or ask for more clarification on what you want to emphasize, in what tone, and length.

Build a Document Interactively

Use Guided Q&A to build a document, step by step.

Sometimes writing feels difficult because you're not sure how to approach or structure your document. One effective solution is to let ChatGPT guide you by using Guided Q&A to ask a series of questions, one at a time. As you answer each question, you can focus on a single answer while ChatGPT analyzes your response and creates a structure and flow for your document.

Based on each response, ChatGPT will shape the next question. By the end, you'll have a complete draft built from your answers. This is easy to set up and is especially helpful when you don't have a clear roadmap for your writing.

For example, imagine you want your company to sponsor your attendance at a conference. You believe the knowledge you'll gain will benefit both you and your organization, but you also realize that securing funding might be challenging. In this situation, building your case interactively with ChatGPT can help you produce a persuasive document that increases your chances of success.

You might start with a prompt like this:

Can you help me write a brief but persuasive request for funds to attend a conference on AI innovation. Please ask me targeted questions, one at a time, and when you have enough information produce a 150-word document.

ChatGPT:

Absolutely—let's build this together. First question:

1. What is the name of the conference, and when and where is it being held?

You:

I want to attend the AI Innovation Conference in Los Angeles.

ChatGPT:

Great, thanks!

2. What are the dates of the conference, and how many days do you plan to attend?

You:

It's a three day conference from June 15-18. I will attend all three days and need a travel day at each end.

ChatGPT:

Perfect.

3. What's your professional role or title, and how does attending this conference align with your current responsibilities or goals?

You:

As a product manager for one of our leading software products, it is clear to me that AI will have a major influence on our product design as well as our back-office processes and customer support. I think we need to understand how AI might change these things so we can remain competitive.

ChatGPT:

Excellent—very clear rationale.

4. Is there a particular session, speaker, or topic at the conference that's especially relevant to your work or that you expect to bring back insights from?

You:

Yes. They are having a workshop for product managers.

ChatGPT:

Great.

5. Will you be requesting funding for travel, lodging, registration—or just the registration fee?

You:

For everything. I will need airline tickets, hotel for 3-4 days depending on schedule. Registration is $795.

ChatGPT:

Thanks.

6. Who are you making the request to (e.g., your manager, department head, or budget committee), and is there anything they care about in particular—like ROI, budget impact, or visibility?

You:

I will ask my manager who is in charge of all our products. She is very sensitive to budget but also wants to be known as an innovator who is up to date with technology.

ChatGPT:

Perfect. I have everything I need. Here's your 150-word funding request:

Subject: Request to Attend AI Innovation Conference

Hi [Manager's Name],

I'd like to request approval to attend the AI Innovation Conference in Los Angeles, June 15–18. As AI continues to reshape product design, internal processes, and customer experience, it's essential that we stay ahead of these shifts—especially in our core products.

This conference brings together leaders in AI and includes a workshop specifically for product managers. I believe attending will help us identify practical ways to integrate AI into our roadmap and operations—keeping us both competitive and forward-looking.

I'm requesting support for full travel and registration costs. The registration fee is $795, and I'd need four nights of hotel and round-trip airfare.

This is a timely opportunity to gain actionable insight and bring back ideas that could directly benefit our product strategy and team.

Thanks for considering it—I'm happy to discuss further.

Best,

[Your Name]

This is a tough request to produce. Using the Guided Q&A technique, ChatGPT generates a solid draft that is concrete and ready for you to review and refine. Asking ChatGPT to present its questions one at a time made it less complicated than if had gotten them all at once, ChatGPT would not have been able to use your answers to shape subsequent questions.

Prompt Template for Interactive Documents

Here is a generalized prompt template you can adapt. It works for almost any situation where you want to build a well-structured document interactively.

- **Can you help me write a [type of document, e.g., persuasive email, proposal, report, etc.] about [brief description of your goal or topic]?**
- **Please ask me targeted questions, one at a time, to gather the necessary details.**
- **When you have enough information, produce a [desired length, e.g., 100-word, one-paragraph, concise, detailed, etc.] [document type].**

Here are instructions for using the template:

- Replace the bracketed sections with your own needs.
- Be clear about the type of document and your goal.
- Specify if you want a certain style or length.
- Let ChatGPT lead the Q&A process and answer each question honestly and completely.

Edit and Improve Your Writing

ChatGPT will edit your writing so it's clear, concise and professional.

Even professional writers rely on editors, and ChatGPT is an excellent one. It can catch errors, improve clarity, and suggest better ways to say what you mean. You can paste in a rough draft and ask for either a full rewrite or a list of improvements. For short sections, a rewrite is often easier to scan. For longer documents, a list of targeted suggestions works best. You can ask for both and choose what to keep.

A useful technique while you're writing is to pause every few paragraphs and paste your work into ChatGPT. Ask for a rewrite. Often, the edited version is tighter. If you prefer it to the original, update your document by pasting in the revised text. With a quick edit, you can turn a rough draft into a polished, professional document, quickly, while retaining your own voice.

Here is a rough paragraph, pasted into ChatGPT. It has good ideas but is not well-written:

> The purpose of this section is to give you an overview of the problem. Also, how it can be fixed. There are a few alternatives: training, a new policy, maybe both? We have to decide what path to take and how much this will cost. Also, who will be responsible for getting it done.

To improve this paragraph, you can ask ChatGPT to edit it so it reads better and is more professional, while preserving your ideas. This prompt will produce both a rewritten paragraph and a list of the changes ChatGPT made:

Please improve this paragraph for clarity and professionalism. Keep it concise but easy to understand. Then, give me a list of suggested edits. [Paste rough paragraph here].

Running this prompt produces an improved paragraph:

ChatGPT wrote:

This section provides an overview of the problem and outlines potential solutions, including training, a new policy, or both. We'll need to determine the best approach, estimate the cost, and assign responsibility for implementation.

The prompt produced a list of the changes that could improve the initial draft.

Here's the list that ChatGPT produced from the prompt above:

1. *Combine the first two sentences into one for smoother flow.*
2. *Clarify the phrase "maybe both?" to avoid ambiguity.*
3. *Use parallel sentence structure when listing options.*
4. *Replace "we have to decide" with a more neutral, professional tone like "we need to determine."*
5. *Specify who "will be responsible" with a placeholder or title if known.*

With this list, you can decide which suggestions to use. You can ask ChatGPT for a rewrite based on the suggested list, address the items raised in the list, or ask it to try again it should read or both.

Specify Editing Goals

You can adapt the prompt to instruct ChatGPT to edit specific elements of your text. Here are examples you can try:

- Improve the tone: "Make this sound more formal," or "Make this friendlier."
- Focus the edit: "Just improve clarity and keep my voice," or "Cut the word count by 30%."
- Create multiple tone and style versions: "Show three versions: businesslike, conversational, and executive summary style."
- Make it sound like you: "Match this to the tone and style of the document that follows: [paste a sample of your writing or any document whose style you want]."

High-quality, professional writing is a powerful skill for influencing others, adding credibility, and establishing your authority. Rather than have ChatGPT produce the initial draft, you can write it without worrying about getting the words and tone exactly right. Then use ChatGPT as an editor to polish your writing so it sounds clear, confident, and professional.

Beat Writer's Block

Turn your vague ideas into structured outlines you can actually use.

Sometimes you just don't know where to begin. When you're stuck staring at a blank screen, ChatGPT can help you get started.

One approach is to use the Guided Q&A technique described earlier to build your draft step by step. But sometimes you don't want to work in small pieces. When the topic is complex, emotional, or high stakes, you may prefer to see the big picture. When you want to go from a blank screen to a complete outline you can review, ChatGPT's ability to organize and expand your ideas can help break the logjam.

This approach is particularly useful when you have a goal or message in mind, but your thoughts feel vague or overwhelming. Turning your ideas into an outline helps you see the structure more clearly. Once you have that framework, your task shifts from creating something out of nothing to refining the rough outline. It's easier and more manageable.

Start with just a topic and a few rough bullet points. Do a mind dump. Don't worry about organization or clarity, just get down ideas as they come to you. This will provide ChatGPT with enough context to focus on what's relevant to you. It will organize your points and expand on them, no matter how chaotic they may seem. Then, ask ChatGPT for a rough outline using bullet points. Use the outline to clarify and shape your ideas. Edit it, remove items you don't want, and add items you do, until it fits your vision.

It won't be perfect at first, but it will get you unstuck. Once you're happy with the outline, you can ask ChatGPT to turn it into full text that you can edit. Example prompt:

- **I need to give a short presentation to our executive team. The topic is why remote teams need better ways to share informal knowledge and how we can address that need. The executives want to focus on low-cost, easy to implement solutions. Can you give me a simple outline, using section heads and bullet points, I can work from? Here are some ideas I have:**
- **We need something like the water cooler for informal communication.**
- **There are timing issues. Remote people may not get together at the same time.**
- **Sometimes you need an answer quickly.**

Here is the output ChatGPT produced from this prompt:

ChatGPT:

1. *Why Informal Knowledge Matters*
   Informal exchanges build trust and shared understanding.
   Critical insights often surface in unplanned conversations.
   Remote work has weakened this layer of communication.
2. *What's Missing for Remote Teams*
   No "water cooler" moment for spontaneous sharing.
   Asynchronous schedules reduce chances for quick check-ins.
   People may not know who to ask or how to surface quick answers.
3. *The Impact*
   Delays in decision-making and duplicate work.
   Missed opportunities to reuse knowledge.
   Lower sense of team connection and awareness.
4. *What We Need*
   Lightweight, low-friction ways to:
   Ask questions and get fast answers.
   Share tips, context, and observations.
   Surface patterns and lessons across teams.
5. *Simple, Low-Cost Ideas*
   Shared "What I Learned" channel (Slack, Teams, etc.)
   Rotating 15-minute drop-in huddles (once a week, no agenda)
   Searchable team FAQ or tips doc (built from past questions)
   Use ChatGPT to summarize or tag shared notes
   Office Hours hosted by team leads or SMEs
6. *Recommendation*
   Pilot one or two of these now—start small.
   Revisit in 30 days to assess participation and value.

Once you have this initial outline, you can edit it, ask ChatGPT for changes (e.g., create a bulleted list under each category), and ask ChatGPT to generate full text or a slide presentation.

Starting is hard, especially when your ideas are fuzzy. ChatGPT's ability to expand ideas and organize information can create the clarity you need. It is always easier to revise when there's something on the page. Your ideas don't need to be perfect or fully fleshed out to get started.

Make Your Writing More Persuasive

Create engaging and convincing messages that resonate with your audience.

Some documents simply inform, but others need to persuade. That's more challenging. You want to connect with your audience and win them over, but you don't want to sound inauthentic or lose credibility.

The real challenge in writing persuasive content, whether it's marketing copy, proposals, speeches, or presentations, is finding the right *tone.* You know what you want to say, but not always how to say it in a way that grabs attention.

A persuasive message needs to focus on your target audience. This means designing the message to address the specific interests, needs, concerns, and motivations of the people you're trying to reach. It requires you to adopt a perspective different from your own. You accomplish this by:

- Using language and examples that your audience relates to.
- Addressing their pain points, questions, or goals.
- Showing empathy for their situation.
- Highlighting benefits that matter most to them.
- Anticipating and answering objections they might have.

Start by stating your core idea and what you want your audience to think, feel, or do. Then, ask ChatGPT to make your message more persuasive, emotionally engaging, and focused on your audience. Experiment with different tones, e.g., friendly, urgent, and confident, to see which works best. Example prompt:

Here is a draft of a product blurb: 'Our software reduces errors in financial reports.' Can you make this more persuasive and relevant to a CFO audience?

Here is how ChatGPT revised the product blurb:

Ensure accuracy, build trust, and protect your bottom line. Our software cuts reporting errors, giving CFOs confidence in every number.

You might follow up by asking for different versions you can evaluate:
Prompt:

Give me two more versions with different tones—one formal and one more conversational.

This prompt, generated two alternatives:

Formal:

Achieve greater accuracy and compliance with reporting standards. Our platform minimizes errors and improves financial oversight at the executive level.

Conversational:

Tired of fixing reporting mistakes? Our tool helps you get it right the first time—so you can stop double-checking and start making decisions.

Here is a *prompt template* you can adapt to make text more persuasive:

Here is my core message: [insert your message].

Please rewrite this to make it more persuasive, engaging, and focused on my audience of [describe your audience—e.g., business leaders, parents, customers, team members, etc.]. Highlight the benefits or outcomes that matter most to them, and use a [choose a tone: friendly, confident, urgent, etc.] tone.

Prompt example:

Here is my core message: Our company should adopt the new collaboration tool to improve productivity.

Please rewrite this to make it more persuasive, engaging, and focused on my audience of department managers. Highlight the benefits for their teams and use a confident tone.

If your document is long, you can paste it in at the end of the prompt or upload it as a file.

Plan and Run Better Meetings

Set agendas, prepare talking points, and follow up.

Meetings bring teams together for many purposes: planning, problem-solving, brainstorming, decision making, culture-building, and getting feedback. But they're expensive. A meeting only delivers value if it leads to clear decisions, next steps, or meaningful change.

Without clear goals, structure, and follow-up, good intentions turn into wasted hours and a frustrated team. Use ChatGPT to help make your meetings focused and productive. We'll suggest prompts for developing a clear agenda, structuring discussions, and summarizing the results as an action plan.

Design a Clear Agenda

Many meetings lack focus and don't lead to well-thought-out decisions or action plans. If you are running the meeting, and control the agenda, you can use ChatGPT to help draft an agenda with time estimates, priority topics, and goals, so everyone shows up prepared.

Her's an example of a prompt you can adapt to create an initial agenda for your meeting:

> **I'm leading a 30-minute project check-in meeting. Can you help me draft a quick agenda with time breakdowns and suggested prompts to keep things on track?**

This prompt produced the agenda below:

ChatGPT responds with a sample agenda:

Opening (5 min): Quick round of updates – what's one thing going well?

Progress Review (10 min): Discuss what's been completed since last check-in

Challenges (10 min): Identify blockers or risks

Next Steps (5 min): Review upcoming tasks and assign owners

Depending on the length, complexity, and goals of the meeting, you can expand the prompt.

Prepare for Meeting Discussion

Whether you are running or attending a meeting, it helps to have clear talking points. ChatGPT can suggest a discussion structure, highlight potential concerns, and propose ways to address them. It can also identify the strengths and weaknesses of different positions. This preparation keeps discussions focused and increases the chances of reaching sound decisions and taking effective action. Here is a sample prompt:

> **I will be attending a meeting where we will discuss our policy on remote work. Can you give me five talking points that support remote work, and explain the concerns, arguments and objections others might have. Present the them as tables.**

ChatGPT responded to the above prompt with the five requested talking points in the following requested table format.

Five talking points in support of remote work

Point	Why it matters
1. Increases Productivity	Studies show remote workers often accomplish more with fewer distractions and less time wasted on commuting.
2. Expands Talent Pool	Remote policies let you hire the best person for the job—not just the closest. This improves diversity and access to specialized skills.
3. Supports Retention & Satisfaction	Flexibility is one of the top drivers of job satisfaction. It helps retain top performers and reduces burnout.
4. Reduces Costs	Fewer people in the office means lower overhead—less office space, utilities, and supplies.
5. Builds Resilience	Remote-friendly teams can adapt quickly to disruptions (e.g., illness, travel, disasters) and keep operations running smoothly.

In addition, ChatGPT produced the following list of concerns and suggestions for addressing them as requested by the initial prompt.

Arguments and objections concerns about to remote work

Concern	Underlying Argument	How to Address It
Loss of Collaboration	"Remote limits spontaneous interaction and creativity."	Propose structured check-ins, virtual brainstorming tools, or hybrid collaboration models.
Weaker Culture & Team Cohesion	"People feel disconnected and loyalty drops."	Highlight ways to intentionally build culture remotely (virtual events, team rituals, shared values).
Uneven Accountability	"We can't see who's working."	Emphasize outcome-based management: clear goals, regular updates, and trust-based performance tracking.
Security & Data Risks	"Sensitive data may be less secure."	Suggest investing in secure tools, training, and policies to manage risk effectively.
Not All Roles Fit	"Some work just can't be done remotely."	Agree—and recommend flexibility: remote where practical, hybrid where needed, in-person where essential.

Summarize Meeting Notes

If you take notes during the meeting, ChatGPT will clean up and organize rough notes into a summary report that captures what was said and the action plan. Don't worry about cleaning up the language. Capture your notes as short, clear phrases, one per line. The trick is to *label* each note whenever possible. Stick to plain language and zero in on facts, decisions, questions, and action items. You don't need full sentences: consistency and accuracy matter most.

The clearer you make who said what, what was decided, and what requires follow-up, the easier it is for ChatGPT to turn your raw notes into a useful, action-oriented summary. Here are examples of quick, structured formats that ChatGPT can easily process.

You may find it convenient to *create shortcuts for labels* that save typing and time, especially if you routinely report out meeting notes. If you are using Word, you can use the Autocorrect function. If you are using Google Docs, there is a similar substitution function. With these functions, you can set a keyboard sequence like "aa" and have it expanded to "Action:" so your notes are clearly and consistently tagged with less typing.

Here is a prompt to transform rough meeting notes into a summary:

Here are my rough notes from the meeting. Can you turn them into a short summary with action items for the team? [paste your notes here]

Table 5.5 A quick, structured format to classify and present meeting notes

Type of note	Format/Structure (Examples)
Assignment	Assign: Jordan to draft a new onboarding checklist by Friday
Issue raised	Issue: Need clarification, next steps or resolution that delays in supplier response are affecting timeline
Suggestion	Suggestion: Automate weekly status reports using templates
Decision	Decision: Move product launch to June 15
Question	Question: Who owns the postlaunch QA plan?
Reminder	Reminder: Schedule stakeholder update meeting next week

AI Meeting Assistants Can Help

Tools like Otter.ai, Fireflies.ai, and Fathom can record and transcribe meetings on Zoom, Teams, Google Meet, or in person. They instantly produce searchable notes, identify speakers, and highlight action items—saving time and reducing confusion. While not perfect, they're worth exploring if you take frequent meeting notes.

Summarize Long Documents

Simplify and extract key ideas from reports and research.

Grasping the core ideas of a long paper quickly is essential when you need insight without getting bogged down in every detail. This is especially useful when reviewing research, evaluating proposals, or scanning dense reports.

ChatGPT can scan and summarize a document, pulling out the key points. This saves you time and is especially helpful when you need to brief others who don't have time you took to read the full text. Reading the summary is another good way to deepen critical thinking skills, by evaluating the key points highlighted or downplayed, "cherry-picked," or how they might be interpreted without reading the whole text.

Summarization is also helpful when starting a new project, and you need to catch up on a large amount of prior work. You might find yourself sifting through cryptic meeting notes, cluttered slide decks, and dense manuals. With information scattered everywhere, making sense of it all can be overwhelming.

ChatGPT's summarization abilities help you get up to speed faster. Upload your stack of materials and ask for a summary of key points. You can request bullet lists, executive overviews, or side-by-side comparisons. You can also ask ChatGPT to simplify complex or technical language, making difficult documents much easier to understand. Example prompt:

> **I've uploaded three research papers on employee retention. Please give me a bullet-point summary of the key findings and note any contradictions or overlaps.**

ChatGPT produces a summary of the main takeaways from each paper, along with a comparison of common themes and differing conclusions. Follow-up prompt:

> **Now rewrite the key points in plain language for a team presentation. Make it simple and engaging.**

ChatGPT generates a clear, audience-friendly version you can copy into a slide deck.

Use ChatGPT to Work with Data

ChatGPT can help you decide what to measure, interpret results, and present them clearly.

ChatGPT can act as a data explainer, helping you spot patterns, summarize findings, and translate technical results into plain language. This saves time and improves how you communicate results, observations or questions the data raise to colleagues, clients, or leadership. These are examples of how ChatGPT can help you:

- Explain metrics and quantitative results.
- Interpret a chart from a description or source data.
- Spot trends or patterns in a table.
- Identify missing information or bias.
- Draft survey questions and summarize responses.
- Write clear summaries for reports or presentations.

The amount of data you can use depends on your version of ChatGPT. **"Plus" users** work best with short, clean tables or lists that can be pasted into the chat. **"Pro" users** can upload larger files with the Advanced Data Analysis ("ADA") tool.

Here are example prompts for Plus and Pro users.

Prompts for Plus Users

Here are example prompts for *Plus Users* that demonstrate what ChatGPT can do with uploaded or pasted tables or lists.

Spot patterns in performance

Here's a table of monthly sales by product. What products are growing, flat, or declining? Suggest one question I should ask about each trend.

Summarize survey results

Here are 50 customer comments about our onboarding process. Group them into themes and write a short summary for my leadership report.

Translate technical metrics

Here are campaign KPIs: CTR, CPC, ROAS. Explain these in plain terms for a client who is not technical and suggest one takeaway per metric.

Identify missing information

Here's a table of project KPIs. What key measures might be missing if I want to evaluate long-term customer success?

Draft Reporting Language

Summarize this revenue table in three sentences suitable for an executive [End prompt text] briefing. Focus on overall trend, best region, and biggest risk.

Pasting Data for ChatGPT Plus Users

For best results with Plus:

- Limit tables to about 30 rows and 8 columns.
- Use short, clear headers.
- Avoid merged cells or long text in cells.
- Paste long lists (e.g., survey comments) grouped and numbered by question or theme.

Advanced Data Analysis (ADA for Pro Users)

ADA is available in the Pro plan. It allows you to upload spreadsheets, CSVs, or text files up to 50 MB. With ADA, ChatGPT can:

- Summarize large datasets.
- Flag missing or inconsistent values.
- Group open-text responses into themes.
- Perform calculations and generate simple charts.

This is especially useful for sales reports, customer feedback, or performance data that are too large or messy to paste into the chat.

Prompt Templates for ADA

The following are prompt ADA templates useful for PRO users.

***Analyze structured data*: "I've uploaded a CSV with monthly sales by region. Summarize key trends, flag missing values, and suggest follow-up questions."**

***Summarize open-ended responses*: "I've uploaded 500 survey comments. Group them into themes, list strengths and concerns, and suggest a report summary."**

***Explore trends*: "I've uploaded an Excel sales report. Highlight key patterns, outliers, and possible risks."**

***Clean and prepare a dataset*: "I've uploaded marketing campaign data. Identify missing values, suggest cleanup steps, and recommend a better structure."**

ChatGPT won't replace spreadsheets or dashboards, but it can bridge the gap between raw data and decision-ready insights. For quick interpretation, Plus is often enough. For heavier analysis, ADA gives you more scale and flexibility.

Using Agents in ChatGPT

Agents complete tasks on their own and return the results to you.

"*Agents*" extend ChatGPT by running tasks on their own, often using connected tools or data. Instead of answering one prompt at a time, an agent can follow a set of instructions, draw on outside sources, and return results when the task is complete.

This means you can delegate routine research, monitoring, or drafting to an agent and free your time. Agents can track information, prepare summaries, or generate tailored outputs such as email drafts or reports. In Chapter 8, we discuss the use of agents for Deep Research.

Agents extend ChatGPT beyond single prompts. Instead of responding only when prompted, an agent runs according to *standing instructions* and can *use connected tools* such as web browsing, file handling, or email. You can create your own agents, add ones from the GPT Store, and schedule them for recurring tasks such as routine monitoring, summarizing, or communication.

How to Start an Agent

To use an agent:

1. Find or create one: Go to Explore GPT (the GPT Store) and either pick an agent or build one by specifying instructions and tools.
2. Define job description and assignments: When an agent is created, the creator sets the agent's "job description." Each time you launch it, you provide task-specific instructions (the "assignment") that supplement the agent's standing job description. Once started, the agent will execute the assignment and return with results.
3. Review results: Check the output, ask clarifying questions, or refine the task if needed.

Agents can search the web. With permission, they can log into websites and extract information. They can also perform actions. For example, if you have an upcoming trip, an agent can find hotels, book a room or make any other reservations you might like.

Agent Example: Daily Industry Brief

Suppose you want a short daily report on your industry. Instead of scanning news yourself, you can set up an agent to scan the web and prepare a summary of relevant news. You might set up the agent so it:

1. Visits chosen news outlets, blogs, and company sites.
2. Extracts 5–8 items relevant to your interest.
3. Summarizes each item, explains why it matters, and suggests an action.
4. Adds a short section on trends or risks to watch.
5. Delivers the report in chat or by email if Gmail is connected.

To create the agent, you would use instructions like:

Track these sources: [list outlets or sites].

Each run:

- **Scan the sources.**
- **Select 5–8 items with clear business impact.**
- **For each, provide a brief summary, why it matters, and a suggested action.**
- **End with a short section on trends and risks.**

Write in plain business English.

Keep the report under 300 words.

If there are no important updates, state that clearly and stop.

Include links to original sources.

Launch Agent Prompts

Here are some examples of prompts to launch an agent:

- **Run today's industry scan and produce the standard brief.**
- **Today, prioritize anything on supply chain disruptions.**
- **Add [new source] to the daily scan starting tomorrow.**

Scheduling an Agent

You can run an agent on demand, or you can schedule it to run at set intervals. To schedule an agent, go to Settings → tasks. You can pause or edit tasks anytime.

Use a *task* such as:

"Run the **Industry Brief** agent every weekday at 7:30 a.m. Email me the result."

(For more information about tasks, consult the ChatGPT Help Center.)

Summary: The Value of Agents

Agents shift ChatGPT from a reactive assistant into a proactive system. Instead of asking the same questions each time, you can set the rules once and run or schedule the agent to do the work when you need the results.

For sole practitioners, this could mean a daily scan for potential clients. For teams, it could mean shared monitoring of competitors, customer sentiment, or regulatory changes. The result is time saved and consistent, structured output.

Build a Custom GPT

Create a repeatable process for yourself or your team.

When you have a process that you want performed in the same way each time, consider creating a Custom GPT. A Custom GPT is a version of ChatGPT set up with *permanent* instructions. These instructions act like a built-in prompt that defines its role, tone, and focus. Every time you use it, it starts from those instructions, so you get consistent behavior without retyping anything.

A Custom GPT is useful when you want the same process, style, or output every time for yourself or for a team. It saves time, enforces consistency, and makes setup automatic.

Custom GPT Example: Sales Proposal Tool

Suppose you lead a sales team and want proposals to follow a standard format. You can set up a Custom GPT to:

1. Begin each session by asking the salesperson structured questions, e.g., customer background, challenges, goals, and budget.
2. Generate a proposal that includes customer summary, proposed solution, pricing, and next steps.
3. Use your company's preferred tone and formatting.

The value of the Custom GPT is that it ensures that every salesperson produces consistent drafts in minutes, while still leaving room for final editing. It can also be used to onboard or train new sales staff.

Here is a sample instruction set that you might enter into the Customer GPT builder, to create a Sales Proposal Tool:

Always act as a sales proposal assistant for [Company Name]. Start every session by asking the user for:

- **Customer name and background**
- **Industry and main challenge**
- **Goals and budget (if known)**
- **Key products or services being proposed**

After collecting this information, generate a proposal with these sections:

Customer background and challenge

Recommended solution

Benefits and expected outcomes

Pricing summary

Next steps

Use a professional, concise tone suitable for client communications.

Custom GPT Limitations

A Custom GPT has the following limitations that are important to bear in mind

1. No memory between chats (though you can ask it to generate a summary or condensed context file at the end for continuity).
2. Can feel rigid if over-specified.
3. Advanced integrations with company systems require technical setup.

Other Practical Details When Using a Custom ChatGPT

- You create a Custom GPT through the *Explore GPTs* tab in ChatGPT.
- You can keep it private, share it with colleagues by link, or publish it publicly.
- Developers can connect Custom GPTs to external systems through an API, but that requires technical knowledge.
- "*Instructions*" are just prompts that never disappear. Use them to lock in repeatable processes or team standards. Custom GPTs are a useful way to get ChatGPT to respond in a consistent, predictable fashion.

Takeaways for Chapter 5

This chapter presents practical techniques for using ChatGPT to make everyday knowledge work more efficiently and be less frustrating. It discusses two ways of interacting with ChatGPT: Ask & Refine and Guided Q&A. Specific techniques suggest ways to speed up routine tasks like writing, editing, outlining, writing persuasive documents, planning and running meetings, and summarizing long documents. Each technique includes examples, prompts, and refinements to help you tailor the technique.

1. Use two interaction styles: Ask & Refine (where you take the lead) and Guided Q&A (where ChatGPT asks you structured questions).
2. Use context to help ChatGPT focus on what is most relevant to you.
3. Use Guided Q&A to draft documents interactively.
4. Ask ChatGPT how it can help you.
5. Edit faster and sound more professional by pasting in rough drafts and asking for a rewrite or improvement suggestions.

6. When you're stuck, give ChatGPT a few bullet points or a messy paragraph, and let it turn them into a structured outline you can refine.
7. Sharpen your message for impact by asking for rewrites that adjust tone, emphasize benefits, or align with audience concerns.
8. Use ChatGPT to draft agendas, prepare talking points, and summarize meeting notes.
9. Ask ChatGPT to summarize dense reports or research into key points, making it easier to grasp the essentials and share insights with others.
10. You can use ChatGPT to interpret data by highlighting trends, condensing insights, and restating technical details in everyday language.
11. A new tool with potentially great power is agents. These turn ChatGPT from just responding to prompts to a tool that can proactively scan the web and execute tasks asynchronously.
12. If you have a process you want ChatGPT to operate in a consistent manner, you can build a Custom GPT, which you can share with a team or the public.

CHAPTER 6

Interactive Conversations

Tell me and I forget. Teach me and I remember. Involve me and I learn.
—Benjamin Franklin

This chapter builds on the Guided Q&A pattern described in Chapter 5. The techniques here go further. Instead of simple questions and answers, you'll use ChatGPT in more dynamic ways to help you think more clearly, solve tough problems, challenge your own ideas, and rehearse difficult conversations.

The techniques in this section are both practical and educational, built on real world situations and cognitive science. People learn best when you can apply and practice skills to act in the moment, and can continue to build on skills you can apply to many situations. With practice and experience, you will become more effective, think more sharply, ask better questions, and handle problems more confidently.

Clarify Your Thinking

Think through ideas by answering structured questions.

We often hold strong ideas that seem useful but are still vague and haven't been fully explored. An interactive conversation helps you crystallize your thinking so you can chart a clear path forward.

This technique uses Guided Q&A to generate *open-ended questions* that help you clarify your ideas, surface assumptions, and identify priorities. As you work through your responses to ChatGPT questions, vague or overwhelming issues become more concrete and manageable.

The result is sharper focus, accuracy, and clarity. It sparks a shift in perspective that ultimately leads to better outcomes. As you gain clarity, you can ask ChatGPT focused questions to deepen your understanding.

How to Set Up a Guided Q&A Dialog

As always, *clarity* and *specificity* in your prompt will lead to the best results. Be explicit. For example, tell ChatGPT:

- What you're trying to figure out.
- That you want it to ask questions, not give answers.
- How detailed or focused you want the questions to be.
- If you want it to respond as if it had a specific role or knowledge.

Here's a prompt template you can adapt:

Help me think through [topic or problem] as if you were a [role. E.g. business coach]. Ask me a series of open-ended, business-focused questions. Don't give advice—just ask questions to help me clarify my goals, challenges, and options. Wait for my response to each question before continuing.

Here is an example of a prompt, built on this template:

Help me think through whether I should leave my current job as if you were a career coach. Ask me a series of open-ended, business-focused questions. Don't give advice—just ask questions to help me clarify my goals, challenges, and options. Wait for my response to each question before continuing.

Here is the flow of dialog produced by the prompt above:

ChatGPT:

Sure. To start: What are the main reasons you're considering leaving your current job?

(User responds.)

Thanks. Next: What aspects of your current job do you find most valuable or satisfying?

(User responds.)

Understood. Now: What would an ideal job look like for you in the next one to two years?

...and so on.

Enhancing Guided Q&A Templates and Prompts

You can alter the words and style of the prompt for your situation. Just be as clear and unambiguous as you can. When the output is not what you expect, you'll get the hang of how much context or specificity is needed. Enhance your prompt by adding elements such as the following:

1. Specify the desired level of challenge:
   "Feel free to challenge my assumptions and push me to consider alternative perspectives."
2. Indicate preferred response format:
   "Summarize key points after every three questions."
3. Time or length constraints:
   "Limit the conversation to five questions."
4. Add a summary request:
   "At the end, provide a brief summary of the main insights from our conversation."

Example of an Enhanced a Guided Q&A Template

Here is an example of an Enhanced Guided Q&A template that incorporates elements in this list:

> **Help me think through [topic or problem] as a business coach by asking open-ended, business-focused questions. Don't give advice—just help clarify my goals and options. Challenge my assumptions where appropriate. Wait for my response after each question, and at the end, summarize the key insights in three bullet points.**

Examples: Prompts for Guided Questions

The following examples are prompts based on an enhanced template.

- **Help me think through a business idea I'm excited about. Ask me thoughtful questions, one at a time, to clarify my goals, target audience, and any assumptions I might be making unconsciously.**
- **I'm planning to propose a new initiative at work but am unsure how to position it. Ask me questions, one at a time, to help clarify the purpose, potential benefits, and risks.**

- **I feel stuck on whether to change careers. Please ask open-ended questions, one at a time, to explore my motivations, concerns, and what matters most in this decision.**
- **I'm leading a project that isn't going well. Can you ask questions, one at a time, that might reveal blind spots or help me rethink my approach?**
- **I have an idea for a training program, but it's still vague. Please ask questions to help me refine the concept, define the outcomes, and identify potential gaps.**

Note that each of these prompts tell ChatGPT to lead the conversation and present the questions one at a time for you to respond to before going to the next question. This technique is extremely valuable because it requires you to consider your response – or even change course – taking you down a different path.

Solve Problems and Build Plans

Use structured dialog to turn ideas into a concrete plan.

Use this structured dialog to initiate a step-by-step conversation designed to help you move from a general goal to a clear plan of action. Use it when you have a destination in mind but need help mapping the most effective path to reach it.

This technique is for *structured problem-solving.* It assumes you already have a goal or decision in mind and need to work through the details. This is less exploratory and more constructive than the previous technique of guided questioning. This approach is useful in situations like:

- You're trying to decide among options.
- You need to outline a plan or process.
- You want help thinking through logistics or trade-offs.
- You have a complex problem and want to break it into steps.
- You want to reduce overwhelm and take one thing at a time.

As the dialog unfolds, it keeps track of the overall structure while you concentrate on each decision or detail. This makes it easier to compare options and spot missing steps.

How to Set Up the Dialog

As always, be specific about the problem and what kind of structure you want. As you write your prompt, avoid ambiguity so ChatGPT's interpretation is clear. There are many options you can request to get the outputs that are most useful to you.

Here is a basic prompt where you only need to specify the project or goal and the output you want:

> **Help me [goal] step by step; ask one question at a time, confirm goals and constraints first, keep a running log of decisions, summarize after each step, and end with [final deliverable].**

Prompt Options

There are many options you can add to the prompt. Here are examples of enhanced prompts:

- **Help me [goal] for [audience/stakeholders] within [constraints].**
- **Ask one question at a time. Confirm [goal, constraints, criteria] first.**
- **Track facts, options, and decisions in a running log.**
- **Summarize each step and state the next question.**
- **Finish with [final deliverable: action plan, timeline, resources].**

Make Changes as You Go Along

One of the most powerful features of Guided Q&A is its flexibility. ChatGPT can shift the conversation at any point based on your responses.

This flexibility allows you to start with a simple prompt and ask for enhancements as you go along. This approach may feel more conversational and helps keep responses manageable and relevant.

For example, you might start with this basic prompt:

> **Help me plan the launch of an online course. Guide me step by step, asking questions one at a time.**

When you start with a simple prompt like this, ChatGPT will plan to ask a series of questions to get the details. For example, the first three questions might be:

1. What is the specific problem or decision you want to work through?
2. What would a successful outcome look like for you?
3. What constraints should I keep in mind—such as time, budget, resources, or skills?

As you enter your responses, you can ask for additional options or completely shift the conversation. At any time—*even before you get a response*—you can say, "Let's scrap this plan and try a new approach."

You can also make smaller adjustments. You might ask ChatGPT for a summary or preliminary timeline, or request that it assess risks. As the conversation unfolds, pay attention to what would make the process more helpful. Ask for outputs or shifts, and ChatGPT will incorporate them immediately. Here is an example:

(ChatGPT asks a question)

You:
Yes, and after each major step, please mention any common mistakes to watch for.
ChatGPT:
Understood. At each milestone, I'll include common pitfalls to avoid. Let's continue—what format will your course take (video, live, etc.)?

Other enhancements you might request are:

- Can you show our steps so far as a checklist?
- Please summarize key risks at each stage.
- Can you provide an example of a project timeline?
- Going forward, after each decision, please warn me about common mistakes.
- Could you provide templates for emails or launch announcements?
- Please suggest relevant software tools at each stage.

- Focus more on marketing strategies from here on out.
- Can you go back and add a section on budgeting?
- Please create a table summarizing all our steps and decisions.
- Make a checklist from our action plan.
- Give me a timeline with key milestones.

Here are some additional examples of prompts using elements from this list.

- **Help me create a disaster recovery plan for our IT systems. Ask one question at a time, verify assumptions, and summarize risks at each step.**
- **Guide me through planning a company retreat. Challenge my ideas on budget, logistics, and scheduling, and keep a running list of action items.**
- **Help me design a customer onboarding process. Start with objectives, then move through touchpoints, resources, and measurement, keeping a step-by-step outline as we go.**

With experience, you'll learn to recognize which enhancements and adjustments give you the most useful results. Over time, you may find yourself starting with a lean prompt and adding structure as the conversation develops—or beginning with a highly detailed setup to get maximum precision from the first step. Either way, the key is to stay actively engaged, guiding the dialog so it produces exactly the plan you need.

Prepare to Defend Your Ideas

Invite ChatGPT to pressure-test your thinking—even the arguments you'd normally dismiss.

No matter how good your ideas are, someone will disagree and push back. How you counter objections determines if your ideas survive and if others support them.

A *Constructive Challenge Dialog* is an interactive conversation where assumptions and arguments are questioned in a respectful way. The goal isn't to "win" but to sharpen thinking, uncover blind spots, surface hidden assumptions, or explore perspectives you might not have considered.

Use the Constructive Challenge Dialog technique when you're preparing for a pitch, proposal, presentation, or any situation where your reasoning might be challenged. By rehearsing with a constructive skeptic who won't let you off the hook, you'll be better prepared for the inevitable pushback. The goal is to expose weak points in your thinking and improve your ability to explain, justify, or adjust your ideas to accommodate valid concerns.

Use the Constructive Challenge Dialog technique when:

- You're preparing for a pitch, negotiation, or proposal.
- You want to stress-test your reasoning before presenting it.
- You're developing talking points or anticipating pushback.
- You suspect your idea isn't fully baked, but you're not sure where the cracks are.

This is especially valuable when you expect real-world resistance from a team member, boss, client, stakeholder, or competitor.

Set Up a Constructive Challenge Dialog

Be clear about what you want ChatGPT to challenge, and what role and tone you want it to take. For example: neutral critic, hostile investor, skeptical client.

This is a sample template for a Constructive Challenge Dialog:

> **I'd like to strengthen my thinking on [topic or idea]. Please ask me probing, open-ended questions that challenge my assumptions, reasoning, and conclusions. Help me clarify and defend my position. Take the role of [someone who disagrees], asking tough questions, raising objections, and pushing me to respond thoughtfully. Ask one question at a time and stay in character until I ask you to stop. '**

Here is an example of a Constructive Challenge Dialog:

> **Challenge my idea to raise prices on our top-tier software plan. Play the role of a skeptical executive team member.**

ChatGPT:

Why now? Our competitors aren't raising prices—why should we risk losing customers in a tight market?

(User responds.)

ChatGPT:

All right. But have we looked at churn data from the last time we raised prices? What makes you confident this won't backfire?

(User responds.)

ChatGPT:

Even if your assumptions are right, what's the plan if we lose 10% of our premium subscribers?
...and so on.

ChatGPT will question you to help surface blind spots and elaborate your ideas. Instruct ChatGPT how tough you want the questioning to be. You might request, "Challenge me gently and focus on major assumptions," or "Be ruthlessly skeptical and press every possible weakness." This helps you avoid overly agreeable output.

Steering the Conversation

If you want to explore the issue from more than one perspective, ask ChatGPT to switch roles. For example, shift roles from a hostile investor to a supportive colleague or neutral regulator. You can shift the conversation at any point. Examples of how to use the Adaptive Steering technique include five concise, ready-to-use mid-dialog commands you can paste in with any response:

1. **"Go deeper on that point and give me more angles."**
2. **"Challenge that answer more aggressively."**
3. **"Switch to a supportive coach and help me refine this."**
4. **"Focus only on practical, actionable steps for now."**
5. **"Zoom out and check if the overall plan still makes sense."**

When you are ready to wrap up, you can ask for a summary:

Highlight any weaknesses you uncovered and suggest ways I can strengthen my argument.

Be aware that engaging with a relentless skeptic can feel uncomfortable or frustrating. If you notice this, pause and remind yourself that the goal is to improve your argument in a safe, low-stakes environment – not to win!

Example Prompts for Constructive Challenge Dialog

If you'd prefer a gentler approach, adjust the wording. Tell ChatGPT to "act as a supportive guide" or "ask open, non-judgmental questions." A lighter challenge can help if you're still shaping early ideas or need space to explore without pressure to go down a path too quickly.

These prompts tell ChatGPT to challenge you and question your assumptions, demand specifics, and make you defend each choice. This approach works best if you already have some expertise or want to stress-test your ideas quickly.

- **I'm proposing a shift to remote work for my team. Challenge my thinking so I can prepare for concerns and objections from leadership.**
- **I believe our marketing strategy should focus on small businesses rather than enterprise clients. Ask me questions to test my reasoning and see if the logic holds up.**
- **I'm planning to cut a legacy product line to streamline operations. Help me defend this decision by asking tough questions about impact, risk, and alternatives.**
- **I want to launch a new service, based on a trend I've noticed. Challenge me on the feasibility, risks, and assumptions before I invest more time.**
- **I'm writing a white paper. Question my assumptions and demand specifics as we define scope, audience, and structure. Keep an outline.**
- **I want a product marketing strategy. Challenge my reasoning on goals, messaging, channels, and timing. Keep a summary.**

You don't have to stick with the same tone for the entire exchange. If the questions feel too intense or not probing enough, you can change the direction on the fly. Tell ChatGPT to slow down, dig deeper on a point, explore alternative perspectives, or focus on practical steps. You might also ask it to switch roles, e.g., from skeptic to supportive coach, from strategic thinker to detail checker, or from big-picture planner to technical specialist. These mid-dialog adjustments can keep the exchange productive while matching the pace and depth you need in the moment. This illustrates how to combine Adaptive Steering with Constructive Challenge Dialog.

Role-Play Difficult Conversations

Practice with ChatGPT before an emotionally-charged discussion.

Role-playing is a powerful technique for practicing challenging interactions you realistically can expect before they happen. By having ChatGPT assume the persona of an employee, a client, a journalist, or a hiring manager, you can rehearse your approach, refine your language, and improve your confidence before the real discussion.

When you ask ChatGPT to role-play, it adjusts its style of interaction to reflect the role you've requested. For instance, if you're preparing to speak with an underperforming employee, ChatGPT can respond as the employee might, raising objections, asking questions, and expressing concerns. This helps you practice framing your words, managing your tone, expressing empathy, and responding to pushback.

Typical examples of challenging business conversations you can rehearse include:

- Addressing underperformance with a team member.
- Negotiating terms with a difficult client.
- Preparing for a challenging job interview.
- Handling sensitive interactions with media or stakeholders.

This technique can also prepare you for tough personal conversations, such as conflict resolution, setting boundaries or asking for help.

How to Set Up a Role-Playing Dialog

To initiate role-playing, simply prompt ChatGPT clearly about the role you'd like it to assume. Here is a role-play prompt template:

> **I'd like you to act as [describe the role, e.g., an employee, a customer, a journalist]. The situation is [briefly explain context]. [Indicate who starts—either I'll start the conversation, or please start the conversation.] Respond realistically, including natural objections, questions, or concerns, so I can practice handling this challenging interaction.**

Decide whether you prefer to start the conversation or have ChatGPT begin. If you start, ChatGPT reacts to your initial approach, using your style to guide the scenario. If you ask ChatGPT to start, it sets the initial tone, challenging you to respond dynamically. In either case, the conversation is shaped by your responses.

Pause to reflect, request feedback on your communication, or repeat certain points until you feel comfortable. Practicing in a safe environment improves your confidence in the soundness of your decision and your ability to handle any twist the actual discussion may take.

Role-playing is most effective when paired with reflection. After a simulated conversation, ask ChatGPT for feedback or alternative ways you could have handled difficult moments. You can also adjust the scenario's emotional tone, requesting a more resistant, emotional, or supportive response, anticipating the situation you will encounter.

Consider switching roles to practice both sides of the discussion. This can reveal blind spots and deepen empathy. Finally, end your practice by asking for a summary of lessons learned and key takeaways.

The following are examples of different role-play prompts:

- **I'd like you to act as an employee who's dissatisfied with recent workload increases. I'm your manager, and I'll start our conversation about workload balance and priorities. Respond realistically, sharing your concerns and frustrations, so I can practice empathetic listening and effective problem-solving.**

- **I'd like you to act as an employee who's been struggling with deadlines. I'll start the conversation to discuss performance and improvement plans. Respond naturally and realistically.**
- **Act as a long-time client who's unhappy about an upcoming price increase. I'll begin the conversation by explaining the reasons for the change. Respond naturally, raising objections and concerns, so I can practice handling this difficult conversation effectively.**
- **You're a strong job candidate negotiating salary and benefits. I'll play the hiring manager, opening with an initial offer. Respond by realistically negotiating for a higher salary or additional benefits. Allow me to practice managing expectations while preserving goodwill.**
- **You're a key team member resistant to a new workflow system being introduced. I'll start by explaining the reasons behind the change. Please respond by expressing your concerns and resistance openly, enabling me to practice constructive conflict resolution.**

Role-playing helps you build confidence and clarity before the actual discussion. Difficult conversations are emotionally taxing and not always received well. By practicing in a safe environment, you prepare a communication strategy, ideas on how to respond to various types of reactions and develop emotional resilience. Rehearsal helps you manage challenging interactions calmly and constructively. It also demonstrates self-awareness and agility in the moment to turn down the heat of confrontation to problem-solving, asking questions to evaluate your assumptions, and perceptions.

Multi-Perspective Framing

Use AI to shape high-stakes messages for audiences with different perspectives.

When you're communicating with a group that includes people from different roles, disciplines, agendas, priorities, or backgrounds, a clear message isn't always enough. What's obvious to one person might seem irrelevant, confusing, or even threatening to someone else.

"*Multi-Perspective Framing*" is a technique helps you anticipate those differences before you write. Instead of guessing what each audience needs, you can ask ChatGPT to simulate a range of perspectives, identify possible misunderstandings, and help you build a layered message that speaks to everyone at once.

Consider this approach when preparing presentations or emails that will be widely distributed. It is also appropriate for proposals and reports for committees, cross-functional teams, clients, or boards. It helps you move beyond tone and formatting adjustments to something deeper: aligning on purpose, priorities, and value, without flattening your message. In a high-stakes situation, you may want to further prepare by rehearsing a presentation by using the technique "*Role-Play Difficult Conversations.*"

Using Multi-Perspective Framing

Here are a few examples of situations where using the Multi-Perspective Framing approach works well. Each includes a short prompt you can adapt to your situation.

1. Team meetings:
   Prepare a message that aligns a cross-functional team (finance, marketing, product, and operations) around a new initiative. Flag any possible misalignment.
2. Client communication:
   Help me draft a summary of our service strategy for an executive client team, including a tech lead, CFO, legal counsel, and customer experience lead.
3. Internal proposals:
   Create a compelling proposal for a new hiring process. It needs to make sense to both HR and engineering leadership.
4. Board presentations:
   Build a presentation outline that speaks to the board's financial, legal, and ethical concerns. Highlight the story first, then the data.
5. Cross-cultural messaging:
   Help me explain a pricing change to an international partner group. Include clarity for readers with different languages and backgrounds.

Using Guided Q&A to Multi-Perspective Framing

The short prompts, shown above, are useful for situations where you want a quick response. But if you have a complex or high-stakes, situation, you may want a more precise prompt. Because there are many variations in how you might construct the prompt, using Guided Q&A makes it easier. You provide basic information in the prompt and then instruct the AI to guide you through a series of questions to build a message that works across roles and mindsets.

The questions that follow suggest elements you might want to include in your Guided Q&A prompt to Multi-Perspective Framing. You can decide how much information to place into the prompt and how much you prefer to enter in response to questions.

1. **Describe your audience:**
   Who are you trying to reach? What roles, disciplines, or mindsets might be in the room?
2. **Clarify the purpose and stake:**
   What outcome do you want? Why does this message matter?
3. **Identify areas of possible friction:**
   What concepts, assumptions, or language might be misunderstood, ignored, or challenged?
4. **Shape a layered message:**
   How can you structure the communication so it starts with shared purpose, then addresses each perspective in turn?
5. **Prepare fallback versions:**
   Do you want to generate role-specific variants to follow up with individuals?

Multi-Perspective Framing Prompt Template Using Guided Q&A

Here is an example of a Multi-Perspective prompt template you can adapt and use to initiate a Guided Q&A session:

> **I want help preparing a communication for a mixed audience. The group includes people from different roles, disciplines, and backgrounds. [List the different participants or audience segments].**

I know a clear message isn't always enough—what makes sense to one person might seem irrelevant, confusing, or even threatening to someone else.

Here's the situation:

[brief description of topic and context]

My goal is:

[what you want the message to accomplish]

The stakes are:

[why it matters if it fails or succeeds]

Please guide me through a step-by-step process. Ask me one question at a time. Wait for my response before continuing.

Help me:

- **Understand my audience**
- **Identify possible misunderstandings based on role, mindset, or culture**
- **Build a message that works across perspectives**
- **Suggest optional role-specific variants for follow-up, if useful**

Here is an example of how to incorporate Guided Q&A to a Multi-Perspective Framing prompt:

I want help preparing for a committee presentation. The group includes people from different roles, backgrounds, and ways of thinking:

- **CFO**
- **Marketing VP**
- **Technical Director**
- **Customer representative from another country**
- **Board advisor**

Here's the situation:

I'm presenting a product redesign plan. I want to build trust and support across all of them, despite their different priorities.

My goal is:

To deliver a message that earns buy-in, reduces confusion or resistance, and aligns everyone around a shared direction.

The stakes are:

If I succeed, we move forward with support and clarity. If I fail, we risk delays, mixed feedback, or hidden objections.

Please guide me through a step-by-step process. Ask one question at a time. Wait for my response before continuing.

Help me:

- **Understand my audience**
- **Identify possible misunderstandings based on role, mindset, or culture**
- **Build a message that works across perspectives**
- **Suggest optional role-specific messages for individual follow-up**

Here is what the dialog might look like:

ChatGPT:

Let's start by understanding your audience.

Question 1:

Can you briefly describe what each of the following individuals cares about most in the context of your product redesign?

- *CFO*
- *Marketing VP*
- *Technical Director*
- *Customer representative from another country*
- *Board advisor*

For each, think about what goals, concerns, or values might guide their response to your message.

Once you reply, I'll help identify any areas of potential friction or misunderstanding before we move on to shaping your message.

You:

(You respond. Even with a partial response ChatGPT will continue.)

ChatGPT:

Thanks. Based on your descriptions, here are possible points of misunderstanding or resistance to watch for:

The ***CFO*** *may question cost, ROI, or risk.*

The ***Marketing VP*** *may care more about brand alignment and customer perception.*

The ***Technical Director*** *may flag feasibility, timeline, or infrastructure concerns.*

The ***Customer Rep*** *may raise cultural fit, usability, or feature priorities from their market.*

The ***Board Advisor*** *may test your alignment with strategic goals, ethics, or long-term risk.*

Question 2:

What is your core message? In one or two sentences, what do you most want them to understand or support?
(and so forth)

The Q&A continues through each stage: understanding roles, clarifying purpose, identifying risks, and shaping a multi-layered message, with role-specific variants suggested near the end.

Takeaways for Chapter 6

This chapter demonstrates how interactive dialog with ChatGPT can sharpen your thinking, strengthen your ideas, and prepare you for challenges. Unlike one-off answers, structured conversations such as Guided Q&A and Constructive Challenge Dialog techniques can create an environment where you can test, clarify, expand and communicate your ideas.

These techniques can be very powerful when used in combination with other templates and prompts for common situations that require greater thought and preparation, e.g., to:

- Solve Problems and Build Plans
- Prepare to Defend Your Ideas
- Role-Play to Handle Difficult Conversations
- Multi-Perspective Framing

Specifically:

1. Guided Q&A helps you surface assumptions and clarify goals.
2. Structured problem-solving moves you step by step toward concrete plans.
3. Constructive Challenge Dialog strengthens your reasoning by anticipating objections.
4. Role-play prepares you for difficult or emotional conversations.
5. Multi-Perspective Framing helps you communicate effectively across diverse audiences.

CHAPTER 7

Project Management Techniques

Those who plan do better than those who do not plan, even though they rarely stick to their plan.

—Winston Churchill

In this chapter, we explore techniques for project management. ChatGPT is not a replacement for dedicated project management tools. But not every project is complex, and you may not be able to call on dedicated business analysts and project managers. When you have a project that is more than a few tasks and less than a formal multiphase project, ChatGPT can help you design the overall structure, break it into tasks, produce timelines, analyze risks, and draft communications plans. With GPT-5, it also gained the ability to produce polished graphics that present tasks and timelines for reports and presentations. This chapter covers techniques to:

1. Create an initial project outline
2. Perform a task analysis
3. Update your project plan
4. Anticipate project risks
5. Draft a communication plan

Create an Initial Project Outline

Turn a rough idea into a structured project plan.

Creating an initial project plan is similar to the technique we discussed earlier for creating an instant outline for a document. It is based on

ChatGPT's ability to expand ideas and add detail. It has extensive projects and project management content in its knowledge base, so it can rapidly expand a project description into a complete project plan. Of course, the project plan it creates will not be precisely tailored to your exact needs, but it will be comprehensive and well-structured. ChatGPT can help you define purpose, identify risks, and draft an overview that gets you started. Once you are happy with the overall project plan, you can ask ChatGPT to perform a task analysis and produce a complete task list for you to edit. You can use a very simple prompt like:

> **Help me outline a project plan for launching a new client onboarding system.**

While that might work adequately for a brief or informal project, you will get better results if you give ChatGPT detailed context, including your goals, constraints, and stakeholders. The more details you provide, the better your plan will be, and the less editing it will need. Here is a comprehensive prompt template you can adapt for your projects:

> **Help me create an initial project plan for [project topic].**
>
> **Here are the details:**
>
> - **Goals: [List the main outcomes you want to achieve]**
> - **Constraints: [List limits such as budget, timeline, resources, skills]**
> - **Stakeholders/Audience: [List the people or groups the project will affect or serve]**
> - **Key Deliverables: [List what the project should produce or deliver]**
> - **Timeline: [State desired completion date or major phases]**
>
> **Please:**
>
> - **Summarize my goals and constraints.**
> - **Suggest logical phases or steps to complete the project.**
> - **Identify potential risks and how to address them.**
> - **Include a simple table showing steps, responsible party, and estimated time.**

Here is an example of this prompt applied to a 6-month project, along with the output that resulted from running it:

> **Help me create an initial project plan for launching a new customer onboarding system. We sell janitorial services to businesses. We want to introduce our customer to the team that will support them, provide them with access to our online portal, and ensure their familiarity with the range of services we offer. Here are the details:**
>
> - **Goals: Introduce new customers to our support team, provide access to our online portal, ensure familiarity with our range of janitorial services.**
> - **Constraints: Six-month implementation deadline; team reports to Director of Operations; internal resources only.**
> - **Stakeholders/Audience: New business customers, customer service team, sales team, Director of Operations.**
> - **Key Deliverables: Onboarding process documentation, welcome materials, training guides, portal access process, feedback collection process.**
> - **Timeline: Implementation completed within six months.**
>
> **Please:**
>
> - **Summarize my goals and constraints.**
> - **Suggest logical phases or steps to complete the project.**
> - **Identify potential risks and how to address them.**
> - **Include a simple table showing steps, responsible party, and estimated time.**
> - **Provide a one-page summary of the plan.**

Sample Output

The prompt produces the comprehensive project plan that follows. Of course, it is not a perfect or final plan, but as an initial draft, it can save you hours and provide you with a document you can build on. (Note: sample output has been lightly formatted to improve readability.)

Project Plan: Launching a New Customer Onboarding System

1. **Goals and Constraints**

   Goals

   - Introduce new customers to their dedicated support team.
   - Provide secure access to the online customer portal.
   - Ensure customers understand the full range of janitorial services offered.

   Constraints

   - Six-month implementation deadline.
   - Project team reports to the Director of Operations.
   - Use internal resources only—no external contractors.

2. **Project Phases**

   1. **Initiation and Planning**
      - Define onboarding objectives in detail.
      - Identify required resources and assign project roles.
      - Gain approval from the Director of Operations.
   2. **Process Design**
      - Map the customer journey from contract signing to full onboarding completion.
      - Develop standardized onboarding steps.
      - Create scripts and templates for welcome communications.
   3. **System Setup**
      - Configure customer portal access protocols.
      - Integrate onboarding workflows into the CRM system.
      - Test system functionality internally.
   4. **Training and Documentation**
      - Train support and sales teams on the new onboarding process.
      - Finalize and distribute onboarding guides and job aids.
   5. **Pilot Program**
      - Run onboarding with a small group of new customers.
      - Collect feedback and make necessary adjustments.
   6. **Full Launch**
      - Roll out the onboarding system to all new customers.
      - Monitor key performance metrics for improvement.

3. Risks and Mitigation

Risk	Mitigation
Delays in portal setup	Begin technical work in parallel with process design.
Staff resistance to change	Provide early training and clear communication of benefits.
Customer confusion during onboarding	Simplify materials and test them during the pilot phase.

4. Task Table

Step	Responsible party	Estimated time (in weeks)
Define onboarding objectives	Project Lead	1
Map customer journey	Business Analyst	1
Configure portal access	IT Specialist	3
Develop communication templates	Marketing	2
Train staff	Project Lead and HR	2
Pilot onboarding	Support Team	4
Full rollout	All Teams	2

5. One-Page Summary

The **New Customer Onboarding System** project will establish a consistent, professional process for welcoming new janitorial service clients. The system will introduce each customer to their dedicated support team, provide secure portal access, and ensure they understand all available services.

The project will be completed in **6 months** by an internal team reporting to the Director of Operations. Work will proceed through six phases: initiation and planning, process design, system setup, training and documentation, pilot program, and full launch.

Key deliverables include onboarding process documentation, customer-facing welcome materials, portal access procedures, and training for staff. The pilot program will allow adjustments before full rollout. Risks such as technical delays, staff resistance, and customer confusion will be addressed through early preparation, clear communication, and simplified onboarding materials.

The outcome will be a smoother customer experience, stronger relationships, and faster time-to-value for new clients.

Customize the Project Plan

The initial project plan is just a starting point. The output is intentionally broad to cover typical project needs, so you will want to adapt it to your situation. Ask ChatGPT for the changes you want. If you find the initial response overwhelming or too generic, ask ChatGPT to summarize the main points. You can ask for more detail in individual phases. If specific areas or tasks are not relevant, ask ChatGPT to delete them. Here are examples of additional modifications you can request:

- **"Prioritize these tasks based on impact and urgency."**
- **"Add a budget estimate for each phase."**
- **"Highlight potential risks for each milestone."**
- **"Suggest tools or templates for managing the project."**
- **"Adapt this plan for a shorter timeline (e.g., 3 months instead of 6)."**
- **"Expand on Phase 2, and include a checklist of deliverables."**
- **"Remove sections that aren't relevant to our company size."**
- **"Create a version for presenting to a non-technical audience."**

You can have ChatGPT revise the plan as your requirements become clearer, helping you build a plan that's useful. Example prompts:

- **I'm leading a cross-channel marketing campaign for our new software product. Help me draft an initial project plan that includes goals, deliverables, major phases, and roles across marketing, sales, and design.**
- **I need to create an onboarding program for new employees at a fast-growing startup. Please help me outline an initial project plan that includes timeline, content development, training sessions, and cross-department coordination.**

Creat a Condensed Context File for Future Sessions

A project is rarely completed in one sitting. It unfolds over time, and plans change as new information emerges. You'll refine and adapt your initial project plan, sometimes in small steps, sometimes in major revisions. When you return to work on the project in ChatGPT, whether you're updating tasks, analyzing dependencies, or creating project communications—you'll want ChatGPT to pick up exactly where you left off, with the right context and tone.

However, when you are in a new chat, ChatGPT will not have access to your project plan or the changes you have made to it. To pick up where you left off, you need to provide ChatGPT with a summary of the information, so it's up to date.

The most reliable way to do this is to create a *condensed context file.* This is a short, structured document that contains the essential details of your project along with any style, tone, or formatting preferences. Instead of trying to remember what to paste into a future chat, you simply paste the condensed context file and start working immediately.

Here's a ready-to-use prompt that will create your file in the right format:

> **I want to save a condensed context file for my project so I can paste it into any future ChatGPT session. The file should include:**
>
> - **Project Snapshot – title, purpose, audience, and one to two sentences describing the project's overall goal.**
> - **Structural Overview – major parts or phases of the project.**
> - **Standing Instructions – ongoing preferences for style, tone, and detail.**
> - **Reusable Elements – any recurring templates, formats, or special instructions.**
> - **Current Focus – what I am working on right now and the next step in the project.**
> - **Format the output as a clean, numbered list with clear headings.**

Save the output from this prompt in a text or Word document. *Whenever you start a new ChatGPT session about this project, paste the condensed context file first, then add the specific task or section you want to work on.* This gives ChatGPT everything it needs to maintain continuity and deliver consistent, relevant results, no matter how much time has passed or how many changes have been made to the plan.

While you may not be familiar with context files, we discuss them in Part 4, where they are used to guide text generation. Generally, if you have large amounts of work on any project, you can ask ChatGPT if you should create a context file so you can seamlessly come back to it later.

Perform a Task Analysis

Expand your project plan into tasks.

Once you have the project outlined, the next step is to expand it into specific tasks. Each task typically includes details such as start date (actual or projected), status (not started, in progress, complete, or blocked), estimated duration, and assigned resources (people or materials). *Tasks* are the basic unit project managers use to track progress and maintain control.

Tasks often have *dependencies*. Some cannot begin until others are complete. For example, you can't review a document until it's written. Mapping these dependencies shows the overall project flow. Within that flow, the *critical path* is the sequence of tasks with no flexibility in timing. Any delay along the critical path delays the entire project, which is why monitoring it is central to effective project management.

Expanding a high-level project plan into tasks and mapping their dependencies can be time-consuming. ChatGPT can draft a task analysis for you, producing a list of tasks and suggesting dependencies. You'll need to review the output to ensure it reflects your intent, but letting ChatGPT handle the first pass can save substantial effort.

You can request any output format, but a *task table* is usually the most practical. Tables are easy to edit, and you can add columns for elements you want to track. For long projects, break the plan into smaller sections, such as one phase at a time. Working in chunks helps ChatGPT generate complete task lists without skipping details. Also, if you are no longer in the original chat where you created the project plan, don't forget to include the condensed context file so ChatGPT can remember the plan. (**Note:** If you forgot to create a context file, you can go back to the original chat from the sidebar and either work in it or create the context file.)

Here is a sample prompt for creating the task list as a table:

- **Take the first phase of this project—Initiation for launching a new customer onboarding system for a janitorial services company.**
- **Perform a task analysis and produce a table of tasks. For each task, include: task name, description, responsible party, estimated duration, and dependencies.**

Running this prompt produced the following output:

Task analysis and Details

Task	Description	Responsible party	Estimated duration (in days)	Dependencies
Kickoff Meeting	Meet with stakeholders to confirm objectives and expectations	Project Lead	1	None
Define Objectives	Document detailed goals for the onboarding system	Project Lead	2	Kickoff Meeting
Identify Resources	Determine staff, budget, and tools needed	Project Lead & Ops Manager	2	Define Objectives
Assign Roles	Clarify responsibilities for each team member	Project Lead	1	Identify Resources
Develop Success Metrics	Establish criteria to measure onboarding effectiveness	Ops Manager and Director	2	Define Objectives
Approve Plan	Secure sign-off from Director of Operations	Director of Operations	1	Success Metrics, Assign Roles

This table format makes task analysis both **manageable and editable**. You can add or remove columns depending on what you want to track—such as start date, status, or risks. By focusing on one project phase at a time, you avoid overwhelming ChatGPT with too much detail and reduce the risk of missing tasks.

Creating a Timeline

Once you've defined tasks and dependencies, the next step is to place them on a timeline. A timeline shows when tasks should begin and end, making it easier to see how the project will unfold over weeks or months.

At this stage, you don't need exact calendar dates. A *relative timeline*—using weeks or phases—is usually best. This keeps planning flexible while still showing how tasks build on each other.

Here is a prompt for creating a timeline as a table:

- **Create a timeline for the *Initiation phase of launching a new customer onboarding system.***
- **Use the tasks already defined in the task analysis and show them in a table with: task, duration, dependencies, start week, and end week.**

Timeline

Task	Duration (in days)	Dependencies	Start week	End week
Kickoff Meeting	1	None	Week 1	Week 1
Define Objectives	2	Kickoff Meeting	Week 1	Week 2
Identify Resources	2	Define Objectives	Week 2	Week 2
Assign Roles	1	Identify Resources	Week 2	Week 2
Develop Success Metrics	2	Define Objectives	Week 2	Week 3
Approve Plan	1	Success Metrics, Assign Roles	Week 3	Week 3

Create Project Graphics

Show stakeholders your project in visual form.

With GPT-5, ChatGPT can create a wide variety of polished graphics that illustrate project tasks and timelines. These visuals are excellent for reports and presentations because they make project structure easy to grasp at a glance.

However, these graphics are not easily editable, which makes them less useful when you need precise, up-to-date tracking. For editable diagrams, you can ask ChatGPT to generate Mermaid.js code. Mermaid.js is a plain-text description of a chart or diagram that can be pasted into Mermaid Live (a free online tool) to create an editable version. This approach is covered in more detail in Chapter 13. Common formats you can request include:

- *Gantt chart*—Horizontal bars showing tasks, duration, and dependencies.
- *Horizontal timeline*—Events or milestones arranged along a line.
- *Vertical timeline*—Events stacked in sequence.
- *Milestone chart*—Only major deliverables shown.
- *Roadmap*—High-level phases with main activities.
- *Calendar view*—Tasks laid out in a monthly format.
- *Progress dashboard*—Visual indicators showing percent completion.

Gantt Chart for Phase 1

Below is a Gantt-style chart generated by ChatGPT from the Initiation phase of the onboarding project we've been using. The Gantt Chart format requested through the prompt shows tasks, durations, and dependencies in a clear timeline.

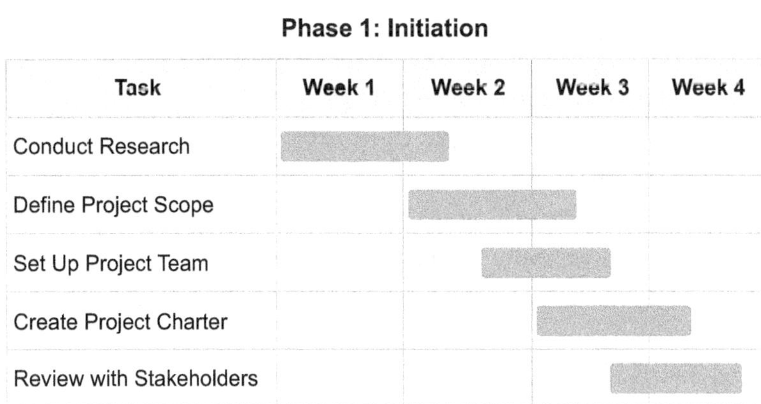

Update your Project Plan

When projects change, your plan needs to change.

Projects rarely go exactly as planned. Deadlines slip, resources shift, and new priorities emerge. Updating your project plan quickly and thoughtfully is key to staying on track. ChatGPT can help you revise your project plan when circumstances change.

It can recalculate timelines, flag risks, adjust tasks, suggest revised priorities, or write updates for your team. Use this technique when:

- A key resource becomes unavailable
- Deadlines change
- Scope increases or decreases
- Stakeholder needs shift
- New constraints or risks emerge

It is likely that updates will occur late in the project, and you may no longer be in the original chat. You can return to it or paste in the condensed context file id you have created one (see the section on Create an Initial Project Plan for instructions).

Then paste in a prompt that explains the changes and requests the output you want.

Sample Project Plan Update Template

Following is a sample template you can use to update ChatGPT of changes in your project plan.

- **I need to update my project plan.**
- **Here's what's changed: [brief explanation of the change].**
- **Please help me [recalculate the timeline | revise scope | flag risks | write an update for the team].**
- **[Paste the condensed context file here, if needed].**

Example prompts:

These prompts assume you have updated the condensed context file or are in the original chat.

- **I've uploaded our current project outline. Our development lead is out for three weeks. What's the revised timeline, and what tasks are now at risk?**
- **Our client just added four new features to Phase 2. Can you adjust the scope and timeline accordingly? Also, flag any bottlenecks.**
- **We lost a developer. Based on the plan below, what can we realistically complete by the launch date, and what should be deferred or reassigned?**
- **Management wants us to deliver the same scope but launch one month earlier. Please revise the plan and recommend tradeoffs.**
- **We just switched to a new vendor for hosting. What parts of the plan does this affect, and what do we need to communicate to stakeholders?**

Anticipate Project Risks

Spot trouble before it starts.

Every project runs into surprises, but most aren't truly unpredictable. When you create a project plan, you typically identify risks and analyze each task for dependencies. But not all risks and dependencies are obvious or considered important to note at points during the planning process.

Hidden risks and dependencies often lurk in assumptions, vague tasks, or misaligned expectations. ChatGPT can help you surface these issues early by walking you through structured questions and analysis. Here are some common examples:

- External approvals (waiting for legal or compliance sign-off)
- People availability (key stakeholder on vacation during a deadline)
- Cross-team coordination (marketing waiting on branding assets from design)
- Technology readiness (can't launch until a server is upgraded)
- Information dependencies (can't write content until the messaging strategy is approved)

You can ask ChatGPT to examine your project plan, identify weak spots, and prompt you to think about what might go wrong. It won't replace formal risk models or critical path tools, but it's a fast, intuitive way to stress-test your plan and fill in blind spots before they become blockers.

Using ChatGPT to identify risks is especially helpful for solo professionals or small teams who don't have the time or budget for formal risk planning. You'll get the best results if you treat risk identification as an interactive conversation.

Working in the original chat or after uploading a condensed context file, as explained in Create an Initial Project Plan, let ChatGPT ask follow-up questions to clarify any details before identifying risks. This interactive process surfaces issues you may not have considered and leads to a more relevant, actionable risk summary.

Prompt template:

Please help me anticipate potential risks, blockers, or hidden dependencies. Before you identify risks, ask any questions you need for clarification, one at a time. Organize your summary by risk category.

Example prompts:

Note: If you use these prompts for a project plan you have created, either work in the original chat or upload a condensed context file.

- **I'm leading a rebranding project for our website. What potential risks or dependencies should I watch for in the design, content, and approval phases? Ask for clarifications before providing your analysis.**
- **I am working on our new customer onboarding system. What could go wrong during implementation, and how can I reduce the chance of delays? Feel free to ask questions before listing risks.**
- **I'm preparing to launch a training program across multiple departments. Help me identify risks related to coordination, rollout, and adoption. Ask me for more information if needed.**

- **I'm planning a product demo event with three external partners. What dependencies might cause trouble, and how can I plan around them? Please check if you need more details before responding.**
- **Please review my plan for switching CRM systems and flag any steps that seem high-risk or dependent on outside timing. Ask any clarifying questions, one at a time.**

Draft a Project Communication Plan

Keep everyone informed, without the chaos.

Clear, consistent communication is often the difference between a smooth project and a stressful one. ChatGPT can help you quickly draft a communication plan tailored to your audience, milestones, and message priorities.

You can describe your project and stakeholders, and ChatGPT will suggest a plan that includes update frequency, channels, and tone. You can also ask it to help you write specific updates or tailor messages to different groups. This is especially helpful if you're juggling internal teams, leadership, and external vendors or clients.

Prompt template:

- **Help me create a communication plan for my project: I need to keep [stakeholder types] informed. Suggest timing, channels, and message focus. Then help me write the first status update.**
- **[Paste condensed context file here, if needed]**

Example prompts:

- **I'm managing a software rollout across three departments. Help me create a weekly communication plan to keep users and managers aligned.**
- **We're launching a new client program. Can you help me plan updates for internal staff, senior leadership, and the client separately?**

- **I need to send biweekly updates on our pilot program. Help me define what to include, and write a short update I can send today.**
- **I'm running a remote project with two freelancers and a senior stakeholder. What's the best way to structure our communication cadence?** [Note: cadence refers to what, how and when communications are provided to stakeholders.]
- **Can you help me create a communication plan for a fundraising campaign that includes donors, staff, and the board?**

Takeaways for Chapter 7

Project management with ChatGPT can save you time constructing an initial project plan, performing task analysis, and tracking progress. It fills a need for project management support for projects that are not complex enough for the overhead of a formal project management system, but are too complex to manage without planning and tracking. By helping you outline, analyze, and visualize your work, ChatGPT reduces blind spots and provides adaptable drafts you can refine. It enables you to iterate quickly, adjust plans as conditions change, and keep stakeholders informed and aligned.

1. Initial project plans turn rough ideas into structured outlines.
2. Task analysis expands plans into actionable steps with dependencies.
3. Timelines and graphics give clarity at a glance.
4. Risk analysis surfaces hidden blockers before they become issues.
5. Communication planning ensures updates are consistent and purposeful.

CHAPTER 8

Strategic Planning

Plans are nothing; planning is everything.
—Dwight D. Eisenhower

In this chapter, we consider techniques for strategic planning. The goal of strategy is to identify and achieve long-term goals, recognizing that the future is uncertain and available information is incomplete. It considers both the external environment and internal resources, aligning goals with actions and decisions needed to move forward.

Many people are more comfortable with tactics than strategy. Both aim to achieve a goal, but tactics are present-focused ("What can I do now?") while strategy is future-focused ("Where do I want to go, and how do I get there?"). The distinction is not always clear and both are important to achieve results.

No one can predict the future, given the complexity of and constantly changing environment or conditions that we may have little control over, be too slow to recognize as significant, or require a major shift from the strategic plan in place and tactical plans underway to achieve.

The true value of strategic planning often lies in going through the process itself to achieve clarity, alignment and commitment to the broad direction and goals to be achieved, and how. The result is a strategic plan that provides both the basis and process for re-evaluation as circumstances inevitability change or play out differently than expected.

In this chapter, we discuss four techniques that support strategic planning:

1. Gain insight through "Deep Research"
2. Brainstorming
3. SWOT Analysis (a commonly used technique for specific decisions that weigh internal Strengths and Weaknesses against external Opportunities and Threats)

4. PESTEL Analysis (a common technique for strategic decisions that extensively review external factors: Political, Economic, Social, Technological, Environmental, and Legal)

Gain Insight Through Deep Research

Use an AI agent to gather and organize information for you.

For quick answers to straight-forward or well-understood issues or decisions a standard prompt is often enough. But quick answers are inadequate for decisions that are less clear, for example, those that are broad scope, have long-term strategic impact, are high-risk, or have significant resource re-allocation implications.

Decisions of this nature require *Deep Research*, extensive analysis of a broad scope of information and well-understood insights that go beyond the surface. The goal of Deep Research is to help you ramp up on a topic quickly and deliver a clear, structured view of complex information.

When you start Deep Research, ChatGPT launches an *asynchronous* agent that works in the background to gather and organize relevant information. Results typically arrive within 5–10 minutes, though more complex topics may take longer.

Deep Research combines ChatGPT's *internal knowledge* with *real-time web searches*, making it especially useful for researching up-to-date topics like product comparisons, company profiles, or market trends. To use it, enter your prompt and click the Deep Research button—or request it directly in your prompt. ChatGPT will update you on progress and deliver the full report when ready.

The output is comprehensive and well-structured, often presented as a report you can review or share. You can also have ChatGPT reformat the results into slide points, summaries, tables, or even a draft white paper.

Areas for Deep Research

There are many ways to use Deep Research. Here are some examples of topics that lend themselves to Deep Research, along with a sample prompt:

1. **Trends:**
   For example: Stay ahead of industry shifts by identifying what's gaining traction and why.

Sample prompt:

What are the top three trends in digital health for the current year?

2. **Competitive Analysis:** Ccompare competitors' offerings to identify strengths, weaknesses, and opportunities.

   Sample prompt:

   Compare available software for internal documentation. Focus on ease of use, integration, vendor stability, customer support, and pricing.

3. **Purchasing Decisions:** Evaluate products or services before committing budget or resources.

   Sample prompt:

   Research the best AI transcription tools for business use. Prioritize accuracy and data privacy.

4. **Emerging Technologies:** Understand new technologies early to spot potential advantages or threats.

   Sample prompt:

   Summarize the current state of quantum computing and its potential applications in logistics.

5. **Policy Scanning:** Track laws, regulations, or industry standards that could affect your work.

   Sample prompt:

   What's the latest U.S. regulation related to AI in education?

6. **Vendor Research:** Assess suppliers or partners to make a selection.

   Sample prompt:

   Find and summarize reviews of the top LMS platforms used by mid-sized nonprofits.

7. **Market Sizing:** Gauge the scale and growth potential of a market before entering or expanding.

   Sample prompt:

   Estimate the current market size for telehealth services in North America and forecast growth over the next five years.

8. **Risk Assessment:** Identify possible risks and ways to reduce or avoid them.

   Sample prompt:

   Identify the key risks and mitigation strategies for adopting AI-powered customer service chatbots in a financial services company.

How to Scope Your Deep Research Prompt

A strong Deep Research prompt gives ChatGPT enough direction to deliver relevant and usable results. You don't need to be overly specific, but clarity helps.

1. Define the topic and goal.
   Sample prompt:
   Research the top AI-powered marketing platforms and recommend one for a small agency.
2. Set priorities or filters: Mention what matters most.
   Sample prompt:
   Focus on affordability, ease of use, and integrations.
3. Specify the output structure: Tell ChatGPT how to organize the response.
   Sample Prompts
   - **Create a short executive summary, followed by a comparison table and a final recommendation.**
   - **Research the top project management tools for creative teams. Compare the top candidates. Focus on collaboration features, design flexibility, and pricing for teams under 50 people. Summarize findings in a three-part structure: executive summary, comparison table, and pros/cons list.**

References to Source Material

You'll typically see ChatGPT show progress while it's researching. Results include source references so you can review the *original source material.* Reviewing the source material is a good idea and sometimes essential to ensure usefulness and credibility of the output. You can also ask for additional source material, for example, that offers conflicting information, or may resonate better with your audience in terms of credibility or expertise.

Deep Research Prompt Template

Here is a Deep Research prompt template you can adapt to your specific needs:

- **Please conduct deep research on [topic or question].**

- **I'm looking for [type of insights or details you're most interested in—e.g., trends, comparisons, risks, case studies, etc.].**
- **This is for [purpose or audience—e.g., internal strategy, client report, product decision].**
- **Prioritize sources that are [relevant filters—e.g., credible, recent, industry-specific].**
- **Organize the results in a clear report format with [preferred format—e.g., summary + sections, table, bullet points, pros and cons, etc.].**
- **If useful, include citations or links.**

Deep Research Prompt Enhancements

The output of a prompt for given to ChatGPT to generate a sample prompt for each of the purposes specified, presented in chart format, is provided below:

Deep Research Prompts

Purpose	Example
Scope constraints	"Focus on [region/industries/company size]. Limit results to the last 2 years."
Market Trends	"Research current trends in [industry/topic]. Summarize the top 3 with examples."
Competitive Analysis	"Compare [Tool A], [Tool B], and [Tool C] for [purpose]. Focus on [key features]."
Purchasing Decision	"Find the top products for [need]. Compare based on [criteria]. Recommend one."
Technology Review	"Summarize the current state of [technology]. Include risks, applications, and future outlook."
Policy/Regulation	"Research the latest developments in [area]. Focus on [region] and summarize implications."
Comparison	"Include side-by-side comparison of top three vendors."
Visuals	"Organize findings in outline form."
Structure	"Include a visual flowchart."

Brainstorm a Strategy

Big-picture planning with practical outcomes

Brainstorming is a technique using an interactive conversation to generate ideas, in this application, for a strategy. Brainstorming is commonly used with others, or in teams, to generate ideas or multiple perspectives, All ideas are collected without debate; if there is strong disagreement, the idea can be flagged for further exploration. [Note: Here we are referring to "brainstorming" between you and the AI.]

ChatGPT helps surface assumptions, gaps in logic, ambiguous objectives, and raise new angles or overlooked factors. You can also use it to model scenarios, weigh trade-offs, and consider how different actions might play out. Because it's fast and nonjudgmental, it encourages the need for exploration

Brainstorming Prompt Template

Using a flexible Guided Q&A dialog, you can shift direction, reprioritize goals, and explore alternative paths as insights emerge. This is especially valuable in domains like business planning, marketing campaigns, product development, and organizational change, where the dialog can surface hidden assumptions to explore.

Here is a prompt template for Brainstorming you can adapt:

> **I want to develop a strategy for [briefly describe your goal, challenge, or project]. Start by asking me a few clarifying questions, one at a time. to understand the context. Then help me [explore options, surface risks, and identify possible steps]. I may adjust direction or priorities as we go, so keep the conversation flexible and responsive. Along the way, summarize key points or decisions when it helps clarify thinking. At the end, give me a concise summary of the strategy—including [main goals, recommended actions, and any risks or assumptions] we discussed.**

Brainstorming Prompt Enhancements

The following are examples of Brainstorming prompt enhancements to specify the format you would like for the summary analysis:

- **At the end, create a decision matrix that compares the main options.**
- **Summarize the recommended strategy in a short action plan with a rough timeline.**

- **Write a one-paragraph summary suitable for sharing with stakeholders.**
- **List the key risks we discussed along with ideas for mitigation.**
- **End with a list of next questions or areas that still need clarification.**

Adaptive Steering: Changing the Conversation

As the conversation progresses, new ideas and insights may emerge. You can instruct ChatGPT to shift direction, reassess priorities, or pivot mid-stream. This technique is called "*Adaptive Steering*".

Here are some suggestions you can incorporate into a response to apply Adaptive Steering to shift the conversation:

- If my answers suggest a change in priorities or direction, feel free to pause and ask if I'd like to shift focus.
- If you notice I'm unclear or hesitating, help me step back and reframe the problem or explore alternatives.
- If I seem to be favoring one direction, challenge my thinking with questions or contrasting options.
- Feel free to point out when a new idea might conflict with earlier goals or assumptions.
- If the conversation stalls or becomes repetitive, suggest a new angle or question to regain momentum.
- Offer to revisit or revise earlier steps if new information changes the context.

These can be included in the initial prompt or entered any time during the conversation, for example: "Yes, and if you notice I'm unclear or hesitating, help me step back and reframe the problem or explore alternatives."

ChatGPT will immediately respond by watching for those cues and adjusting its questioning or suggestions accordingly.

Adaptive Steering is a powerful and underused aspect of working with ChatGPT that can be used, not just for brainstorming, but for any situation that raises questions or ideas that you may not have thought of before, or would like to take in another direction.

Here is an example of how you would use Adaptive Steering, starting with a prompt and output:

I need to increase our customer retention rate by 15% over the next quarter. What strategic options should I consider? Please ask me targeted questions, one at a time, to understand the situation. After gathering enough context, recommend three strategic pathways and briefly evaluate each.

Here is the conversation that results :

ChatGPT:

Great—let's start by understanding your current situation so I can tailor recommendations that make sense for your context.

First question:

What is your current customer retention rate, and how is it measured (e.g., over 30 days, 90 days, annually)?

You:

We have consulting clients. We hope to get follow-on business within 90 days of the completion of a project.

(The structured dialog continues, using adaptive steering to explore points raised or new ideas that emerge.)

At the conclusion of a lengthy dialog ChatGPT identifies the insight that the underlying problem stems from the lack of a process that connects with the customer at the right point following an assignment. It then suggests three strategic pathways to explore:

ChatGPT:

1. Proactive Post-Project Engagement

What it is: Formalize a structured follow-up process after project delivery—such as a 30-day insights report, a "next steps" roadmap, or a scheduled check-in.

Pros:

Positions your team as long-term partners, not one-time vendors

Keeps you top of mind when new needs arise

Cons:

Requires coordination and mindset shift across delivery and sales teams

2. Retention-Driven Service Packaging

What it is: Reframe your offerings into phased services or annual packages with strategic check-ins or advisory add-ons.

Pros:

Makes re-engagement easier for the client (no new proposal needed)

Builds predictable revenue

Cons:

May require redefining deliverables and repackaging internal workflows

3. Trigger-Based Recontact Strategy

What it is: Set up reminders or marketing automation tied to project timelines (e.g., 60-day nudge email, client-specific use-case prompts, quarterly insights briefings).

Pros:

Doesn't rely on client initiative

Low-cost way to spark repeat business conversations

Cons:

Less effective without personalization

You can then explore these ideas in more detail. ChatGPT can help develop templates, messages, or offers for the selected options.

Brainstorming Prompts Examples for Specific Situations

As mentioned above, brainstorming is widely used to explore ideas on a wide range of issues, often in conversations with colleagues. The sample prompts that follow illustrate the wide range of topics you can explore brainstorming in a ChatGPT dialog.

Product Launch

We are planning to launch a new service package for small business clients. Ask clarifying questions about my market and offering, then help me brainstorm pricing, positioning, and go-to-market tactics. If the ideas start to overlap or stall, help me step back and refocus. Finish with a summary of key recommendations and a timeline sketch.

Personal Brand

I want to clarify my personal brand and positioning as a freelance designer. Ask me questions about my work, clients, and goals, and help me explore different positioning strategies. If my answers are unclear, feel free to challenge or reframe them. At the end, give me a one-paragraph brand positioning statement and a few steps to validate it.

Strategic Pivot

We're rethinking our business model after a tough quarter. Start by helping me identify key challenges and opportunities, then work with me to explore new strategic directions. If my priorities shift mid-conversation, follow along and help me adapt. Summarize the most viable path forward, with pros, cons, and suggested next steps.

Time Management Strategy

I'm struggling to balance client work, marketing, and admin tasks. Ask me questions about how I'm currently spending my time, then help me design a more effective strategy. If you see a pattern or conflict, point it out. End with a summary of recommendations and a list of small changes I can test this week.

Grow a Consulting Practice

I want to develop a strategy to grow my consulting practice over the next 12 months. Start by asking a few clarifying questions about my services, clients, and goals. Then help me explore options for

expanding visibility, building client relationships, and increasing revenue. At the end, summarize the recommended strategy and include a short action plan.

SWOT Analysis

Create strategy based on a snapshot of both internal and external conditions that both support or inhibit viability.

SWOT is a common strategic analysis technique used to assess a specific situation quickly. SWOT is an acronym for *internal* **S**trengths and **W**eaknesses and *external* **O**pportunities and **T**hreats. Strengths and Opportunities are perceived *positives* while Weaknesses and Threats are perceived as potential *barriers.*

SWOT is especially useful for relatively narrow strategic decisions, for example, to develop a new product, enter a new market or improve performance. It lends itself well to interactive discussion, which is exactly the kind of situation for which ChatGPT can be very helpful.

It is intended to *quickly* see a high level view of pros and cons of a 2 x 2 chart of bullet points for ease of comparison of *perceived or known*: Internal Strengths (e.g, capabilities, resources) against External Opportunities (e.g., trends, situations to capitalize on); alongside a similar bulleted list of *perceived or known* Internal Weaknesses (e.g., gaps, vulnerabilities) against External Threats (e.g., risks, barriers).

Using ChatGPT for SWOT Analysis

While you may be familiar with using SWOT analysis in a group or team setting, in this context, you are doing the analysis yourself, interacting with the AI. You can use ChatGPT to support SWOT analysis by initiating an interactive conversation. Rather than jumping into the question, start by describing your organization, market, or project. Remember, the greater clarity and context you provide, the better for the conversation to generate a list for each of the four SWOT dimensions.

Once you have a list for each single dimension, you can refine them by prompting for examples, asking follow-up questions, or adding your own ideas. To explore a specific quadrant (e.g., identifying external Threats), ask questions to dig deeper.

When you are satisfied with each of with the analysis, ChatGPT can help build an action plan by proposing strategies for each quadrant.

Prompt Template for SWOT analysis:

Here is an example of a prompt template, the resulting output and conversation.

- **I'd like to perform a SWOT analysis for [company | project | product | idea].**
- **Please help me identify the main strengths, weaknesses, opportunities, and threats.**
- **Here is some background to get started:**
- **[brief context – e.g., company goals, target market, current performance, competitive landscape].**
- **Ask any clarifying questions you need before creating the SWOT. Ask me questions one at a time.**
- **Once you have enough context, present the results in a four-four-quadrant SWOT Table, labeling each quadrant.**
- **I'd like to create a SWOT analysis for a mobile cleaning service that targets small office buildings. We use eco-friendly products, offer flexible scheduling, and rely on a small but reliable team. Please create a SWOT analysis with bullet points under each of the four categories: Strengths, Weaknesses, Opportunities, and Threats. If you need clarification before starting, feel free to ask targeted questions one at a time.**

ChatGPT:

Before I begin, could you tell me more about your competitors and current growth goals?

(The clarifying questions continue)

Once the clarifying questions are answered, ChatGPT produces a SWOT analysis.

ChatGPT:

Strengths

Eco-friendly products appeal to health- and sustainability-conscious clients

Flexible scheduling accommodates client needs outside business hours

Personalized service due to small, consistent team

Low overhead from mobile service model (no facility costs)

Strong customer loyalty from consistent quality

Weaknesses

Limited staffing may restrict growth or capacity for large accounts

Reliance on a small team increases risk if someone is unavailable

Less brand recognition compared to larger commercial cleaning services

Marketing and client acquisition may be underdeveloped

No formal system for client feedback or upselling

Opportunities

Growing demand for green and health-focused cleaning solutions

Partnerships with property managers and coworking spaces

Upsell deeper or specialty cleaning (e.g., carpets, windows, sanitation)

Expand to weekend or emergency cleaning services

Build a referral program to leverage existing clients

Threats

Intense competition from national and local cleaning companies

Price sensitivity among small businesses

Potential regulatory changes around eco-friendly chemical use

Staff burnout or turnover due to physical demands

Economic downturns may reduce discretionary spending on cleaning

You can use follow-on prompts to explore connections across categories.

Here is an example of a general prompt for further exploration to explore connections, inconsistencies, or raise areas of potential conflict or support when looking across categories:

- **Based on this SWOT analysis, how can our strengths be used to counter or minimize the key threats?**
- **Which weaknesses are most likely to interfere with the opportunities we identified?**
- **Are there any strengths and opportunities that reinforce each other and could be leveraged together?**

Other examples of prompts that could be useful are to:

1. Prioritize Issues
   Looking at this SWOT, which threats and weaknesses seem most urgent or impactful to address first?
   Can you rank the opportunities by potential value and ease of execution? Which single factor—positive or negative—should be our top strategic focus right now, and why?
2. Suggest Strategic Responses
   What strategic initiatives could help us neutralize the top two threats? Based on our strengths and opportunities, what's a high-impact move we could make in the next quarter?
   Suggest two or three strategic directions that align with our current position and external landscape.
3. Improve Weak Areas
   What are some practical ways to reduce or mitigate the most limiting internal weaknesses?
   Can you suggest processes, partnerships, or tools that would help us turn a weakness into a strength?
   How could we build internal capabilities to better take advantage of our most promising opportunity?

Prompt Examples for SWOT Analysis for Specific Strategies

For illustrative purposes, we created sample prompts for a SWOT analysis for three strategic decisions:

1. Marketing strategy for a new product launch
2. Internal operations review for a growing agency
3. Consideration of a strategic partnership opportunity

Marketing Strategy for a New Product Launch

- **I'd like to perform a SWOT analysis for a new productivity app we're planning to launch next quarter.**
- **Please help me identify the main strengths, weaknesses, opportunities, and threats.**
- **Here is some background to get started: the app targets remote teams, includes task tracking and integrated video check-ins, and we're competing with tools like Asana and Trello. Our goal is to build market share in mid-sized tech firms. Our beta feedback has been positive but our brand awareness is low.**
- **Ask any clarifying questions you need before creating the SWOT. Ask me questions one at a time.**
- **Once you have enough context, present the results in a four-part table. Then suggest two marketing angles that play to our strengths and opportunities.**

Internal Operations Review for a Growing Agency

- **I'd like to perform a SWOT analysis for our digital marketing agency as we scale from 10 to 25 employees.**
- **Please help me identify the main strengths, weaknesses, opportunities, and threats.**
- **Here is some background to get started: We specialize in SEO and content marketing for professional services firms. We've doubled revenue in the past 18 months**

but are starting to see workflow bottlenecks and team burnout. We're also considering a shift to value-based pricing.

- **Ask any clarifying questions you need before creating the SWOT. Ask me questions one at a time.**
- **Once you have enough context, present the SWOT in a four-part table. After that, prioritize the top three internal issues we should address in the next 90 days.**

Evaluating a Strategic Partnership Opportunity

- **I'd like to perform a SWOT analysis for a potential partnership between our HR tech startup and a national training provider.**
- **Please help me identify the main strengths, weaknesses, opportunities, and threats.**
- **Here is some background to get started: We offer AI-based onboarding and skills assessments. They offer leadership development programs for mid-level managers. The idea is to co-market bundled services to enterprise clients. Our sales cycles are long, and our buyer personas may not fully align.**
- **Ask any clarifying questions you need before creating the SWOT. Ask me questions one at a time.**
- **Once you have enough context, present the SWOT in a four-part table. Then tell me whether the potential benefits outweigh the risks—and why.**

PESTEL Analysis

Extensive but concise analysis on external factors to be considered that significantly influence short and long term strategic decisions.

PESTEL is an acronym for a commonly used framework for analyzing factors in the **external** environment requiring extensive strategy research and analysis that decision makers use to understand, assess and evaluate develop longer-term strategies.

PESTEL stands for **P**olitical, **E**conomic, **S**ocial, **T**echnological, **E**nvironmental, and **L**egal factors. We use PESTEL here because it is well-known and illustrates how ChatGPT can be used and adapted to any framework. It grew out of PEST (Political, Economic, Social, Technological) and evolved as other factors became increasingly relevant.

Other acronyms (regardless of how they are spelled) that you may run into include additional factors, but they all incorporate PESTEL:

STEEPLE: PESTLE + Ethical (or sometimes Ethical/Ecological) factors

PESTLIED: PESTLE + International + Demographic factors

DEEPLIST: PESTLE + Ecological + Informational factors

Getting Started

ChatGPT can develop PESTEL analyses with a straightforward prompt, which you can make interactive for more focused results.

Prompt Template to Initiate a PESTEL analysis:

I'd like to conduct a PESTEL analysis for [industry, company, or product]. The business operates in [geographic region or market]. Please identify key trends, risks, and opportunities under each of the six categories: Political, Economic, Social, Technological, Environmental, and Legal. Use concise bullet points. If any category is not relevant, you may briefly note that.

Using Deep Research for PESTEL

In some circumstances, you may want to use Deep Research (discussed earlier) for PESTEL analysis. The table below was generated by ChatGPT in response to a simple prompt asking for situations ChatGPT suggested that Deep Research would be valuable and why.

Situations Where ChatGPT Deep Is Valuable for PESTEL analysis

Situation	Why Deep Research Is Valuable
New or Emerging Markets	Built-in data may be outdated or incomplete. Deep Research helps provide inclusion of current political, legal, and economic conditions.
Fast-Changing Environments	In volatile industries (e.g., AI, crypto, health tech), regulatory and economic factors shift quickly. Web-based sources help track changes in real time.
International Expansion	When entering unfamiliar countries, Deep Research pulls localized data on laws, political stability, consumer behavior, and economic conditions.
Sector-Specific Trends	If you're operating in a niche (e.g., renewable packaging, space tech), you'll need recent regulatory updates, environmental pressures, or public sentiment.
Due Diligence or Investment Evaluation	For high-stakes decisions, Deep Research provides up-to-date insights for risk analysis and stakeholder presentations.
Competitor or Country Comparison	Comparing environments across regions (e.g., U.S. vs. EU data protection laws) benefits from real-time web data.

Sample Template for Deep Research Analysis

Here is a template for a Deep Research PESTEL analysis:

- **Please conduct a Deep Research PESTEL analysis for [project, product, service, or market] in [industry or location].**
- **Focus on any recent changes, major risks, or opportunities in each category. Present the findings in a table organized by the six PESTEL categories: Political, Economic, Social, Technological, Environmental, and Legal.**
- **Cite recent sources where appropriate. If possible, include region-specific insights and data relevant to decision-making.**

For more precision, you can append any of these to the end of the prompt:

- Include three bullet points under each category.
- Highlight the top two risks and opportunities at the end.

- Summarize key implications for our business strategy in 100 words.
- Focus especially on [factor], since it is most critical for our market.

As always, the more context, specificity and clarity you are looking for will lead to a better results.

Example of a Simple PESTEL Analysis

PESTEL analyses are usually quite extensive but we are keeping it simple for illustrative purposes, with the following prompt and output.

I'd like to perform a Deep Research PESTEL analysis for a janitorial services company expanding into healthcare facilities in the U.S. We use eco-friendly cleaning products and plan to target small medical offices and clinics. Please organize your analysis under the six PESTEL categories. If you need clarification, ask me one question at a time before you begin.

ChatGPT:

Report (Using Deep Research)

Subject: Eco-Friendly Mobile Cleaning Services

U.S. Market Outlook (Q2 2025)

Political

Federal and state governments continue to support sustainability through grants and tax credits for green-certified businesses.

Local ordinances in cities like New York, San Francisco, and Seattle increasingly restrict noise levels and emissions for mobile equipment, affecting service operations.

Variability in local regulations for chemical disposal and water runoff requires region-specific compliance planning.

Economic

Many small offices are outsourcing cleaning services to cut internal costs—boosting demand for affordable, flexible vendors.

Inflation continues to raise prices of eco-friendly cleaning supplies by 4–7% YoY.

Labor costs have increased in many metro areas due to minimum wage hikes and competition from other gig-economy employers.

High fuel prices and vehicle maintenance costs affect mobile team profitability unless routes are optimized.

Social

Employee and client preferences are shifting toward visibly sustainable practices, especially in urban and wellness-conscious office spaces.

Work-from-home flexibility means fewer cleanings are needed weekly, but more on-demand deep cleans are requested.

There is growing preference for companies that market health-conscious cleaning—reducing allergens and harmful residues.

Technological

Emerging platforms like Sweeply and CleanGuru are improving route optimization, scheduling, and customer retention through built-in CRMs.

New battery-powered, low-noise cleaning equipment reduces disruption during business hours and improves compliance with local sound ordinances.

AI-enabled inventory tracking helps reduce waste and restocking costs for small operations.

Environmental

New EPA standards may soon mandate reduced chemical emissions for all cleaning products used commercially.

Drought conditions in western U.S. have sparked new restrictions on water-intensive cleaning techniques.

Consumers and B2B clients increasingly ask for documentation on sustainability practices—offering competitive advantage to certified vendors.

Legal

Revised OSHA standards emphasize ergonomic safety, including the use of lightweight and low-vibration equipment.

Ongoing debate and enforcement around contractor vs. employee classification, especially in California and Massachusetts—pose risks to flexible staffing models.

Non-compliance penalties for mislabeled chemicals or improper storage | disposal continue to rise, particularly in high-density states.

Generating Scenarios

Following a PESTEL analysis, you can ask ChatGPT to generate scenario analyses that describe how external trends might unfold. Each scenario highlights different risks, opportunities, and strategic responses. This is especially useful for planning under uncertainty or preparing backup strategies.

Example prompt:

Based on the PESTEL analysis of our expansion into healthcare janitorial services, please create three plausible future scenarios for the next 12–18 months. Each scenario should show how external trends—like labor shortages, new regulations, or client expectations—might evolve. For each scenario, summarize the potential impact on our business and suggest how we should prepare.

Takeaways for Chapter 8

ChatGPT can help you think systematically about long-term goals in the face of uncertainty. By combining techniques such as deep research amd brainstorming dialogs to frameworks such as SWOT and PESTELs, you can plan based on an assessment of internal and external factors, for both straight forward or complex strategic plan.

While plans often change because of factors outside your control, the process of planning helps you understand trends, question assumptions, compare alternatives, and set priorities. This helps you both in the short term or to revisit to see if and how these changes can affect your plan, how and what to communicate, and keep everyone aligned. This enables you to move forward in an organized way and respond with resilience when the situation changes.

1. Deep Research quickly builds a structured understanding of complex topics.
2. Brainstorming uncovers hidden assumptions and alternative paths.
3. SWOT: analysis, which but can be influenced by assumptions or perceptions, balances internal realities with external conditions to hone in on viable solutions to problems that may have strategic impact, but a tactical focus may be more immediately needed.
4. PESTEL analysis which can also be influenced by assumptions or perceptions, highlights macro-level forces that shape your broader or long term strategic plans and options.
5. The process of strategic planning itself improves adaptability and decision-making.

CHAPTER 9

Learn New Concepts and Skills

The capacity to learn is a gift; the ability to learn is a skill; the willingness to learn is a choice.

—Brian Herbert

ChatGPT can help you build knowledge and skills for many purposes—preparing for important meetings, priming your thinking before new projects, understanding emerging technologies that affect your business, or strengthening your overall professional competence so you take on new assignments and continue to grow. Drawing from its extensive knowledge base, ChatGPT can personalize both instruction and practice to your needs.

Learning involves both knowledge and skills. Gaining *knowledge* means understanding new ideas or theories. Whether you want to explore a new subject or deepen your expertise in a familiar one, ChatGPT can provide explanations, examples, and answers to clarify and expand your thinking and curiosity. Building or improving *skills* requires structured, continuous practice and feedback. ChatGPT can guide you step by step, offer practice scenarios, and give constructive critiques. It may seem hard to find the time but you're likely to find that it will pay off in terms of honing critical thinking, problem solving and communication skills, especially when circumstances change and agility becomes important.

Here are some examples of how you might use ChatGPT for learning:

1. If you are meeting a new client, preparing for a sales call or job interview, use ChatGPT to brief you on the basics of their business, industry, successes and challenges.

2. If you are on a team or asked to come up with strategies for an important decision, use ChatGPT to explore how strategic analysis is done.
3. If you want to build your communication skills, use ChatGPT to help you learn how to structure persuasive communications, gain multiple perspectives, role-play or to create writing exercises for you and give you feedback on your responses.
4. If you want to explore new technology, use ChatGPT to guide you through the basics or provide step-by-step instructions so you can experiment with it.

Acquire New Knowledge

Cain quick familiarity or explore a topic deeply. Learn more or update yourself on topics you think you know. Find out what you don't know.

In this section, we'll look at two ways to engage ChatGPT as a tutor. The first uses the Ask & Refine approach, while the second uses Guided Q&A to engage you in a Socratic dialog. Of course, you can mix these techniques and experiment in any way that works for you. *Most important is actively connecting new material to the knowledge you already have.* That is what builds understanding, enables you to apply what you learn confidently and expand new knowledge to solve problems, take on harder challenges and stimulate ideas for innovating new solutions.

Using Ask & Refine to Expand Your Knowledge

When you want to explore a new area of knowledge, use a prompt that gives you an overview, examples, and interactive questions to test your understanding. Here is a prompt template using the Ask & Refine technique:

> **I'd like to understand [concept or topic] in a clear and practical way. Please explain it concisely, include relevant examples, and ask me one or two clarifying questions to check my understanding or tailor the explanation further.**

Follow up by asking for more detail to explore responses more deeply to make sure you have mastered the topic correctly and sufficiently for your situation. Here are example prompts:

- **I'd like to understand the difference between market penetration and market expansion strategies. Explain each clearly, provide practical business examples, and ask questions to help ensure I understand.**
- **I'd like to learn about cash flow management. Explain why it's important, provide a simple example relevant to freelancers, and ask a clarifying question to test my comprehension.**
- **Help me understand how the Five Forces model works. Clearly explain the key elements, illustrate with an example from a service industry, and ask me one or two questions to confirm my grasp of the framework.**
- **Teach me about compound interest. Ask a few questions and give me one problem to solve.**
- **Teach me the basics of Excel formulas. Explain SUM, AVERAGE, and IF functions in simple terms. Then ask me a few questions to check my understanding and give me one small spreadsheet scenario to practice with.**
- **Help me understand how supply and demand affect pricing. Explain the concept clearly, walk me through a simple example, and ask me a few questions to confirm I understand the relationship. Then give me a real-world situation to analyze.**
- **Teach me how to write a project summary. Explain what a good summary includes, show me an example, and ask me to rewrite a short paragraph in summary form. Then give me feedback on how I did.**

After you submit your prompt, ChatGPT will respond with a concise yet comprehensive explanation, practical examples relevant to your request, and targeted clarifying questions to confirm your understanding. You can then respond, ask follow-up questions, or request further examples to deepen your grasp of the concept.

For example:

- Ask for analogies, timelines, or visual explanations.
- Use ChatGPT to quiz you after a learning session.
- Ask ChatGPT to combine with summarizing articles or extracting key terms. (Remember to ask for source references!)

Follow-Up Prompts to Deepen Understanding

With greater knowledge, practice and experience you'll ask increasingly better questions, including if others might answer a question differently if they had a different perspective.

Here are some follow up prompts you can use to deepen your understanding:

- **Give me more detail about [topic], especially the parts most relevant to [my industry | my role | a specific situation].**
- **Use an analogy to help me better grasp [topic].**
- **Create an infographic or diagram about [topic] so I can visualize the key ideas.**
- **Give me a timeline of how [topic] developed.**
- **Show me a timeline of how [topic] is typically implemented.**
- **Create a short quiz to test my understanding of [topic] and give me feedback.**
- **Summarize [topic] in one paragraph I could use to explain it to a colleague.**
- **Compare [topic] to [another topic] so I understand the difference.**
- **List a few common misconceptions about [topic] and provide valid, accurate information.**
- **Suggest ways I could apply [topic] in my current work.**
- **What should I learn next if I want to go deeper into [topic]?**

The Ask & Refine prompt templates shown earlier are designed for speed, clarity, and relevance. They work well for many situations by delivering a brief, focused explanation with just enough interactivity to ensure you're on the right track.

Using Socratic Dialog for Deeper Learning

Ask & Refine is very useful for quick overviews, validating answers you receive in the output, and a little digging below the surface. But it stops short of a true Socratic dialog, which is useful when you want to learn an area more deeply and gain more insight than the quick prompt supports.

"*Socratic Dialog*" is a teaching style identified with the Greek philosopher Socrates. It leads the learner to insight by answering questions. As you answer and reflect on them, you build a *mental model* of the topic that supports deep learning. Mental models may not be a familiar term to you, and understanding it fully goes beyond the scope of this book. In overly simplistic terms, mental models are ways of looking at the world and how things work, for example, that you learn and come to know intrinsically.

Socratic dialog is a more exploratory method upon which the the Guided Q&A technique was built. Instead of explaining a concept as with a single, standard prompt, ChatGPT leads you through a series of questions designed to reveal your assumptions, test your understanding, and help you reason through the topic step by step.

It's slower and more reflective, but more powerful when you want to learn something deeply or think more critically.

Sample Prompt Template for Socratic-Style Dialog

Using this method, you are likely to ask questions you may not have thought to ask initially that leads to another. This is a quick explanation of how the Guided Q&A technique can help you acquire deeper knowledge and critical thinking (e.g., distinguishing fact from fiction, evaluating the relevance of information, the ability to logically explain your conclusions.)

Here's a prompt template to start a Socratic-style conversation:

> **I'd like to understand [concept or topic] more deeply. Instead of just explaining it, please guide me through a series of questions—like a Socratic dialoge—that will help me uncover the key ideas and test my assumptions. Offer brief answers or nudges as needed, but let's focus on building my understanding through the questions.**

This approach works especially well when you're willing to slow down and think out loud, in this case with ChatGPT. *It mirrors the kind of exploratory thinking that leads to lasting insight.* ChatGPT is well-suited to support it, without ego, judgment, or agenda. It's not insulted if you ask why it answered the way it did, to provide you with opposing views, or show you the evidence for output. In short, this is one example of how AI can make you smarter!

Brief Example of a Socratic Style Interaction

Building on this prompt template, following is a prompt and the resulting dialog that illustrates a Socratic-style interaction.

> **I'd like to understand opportunity cost more deeply. Guide me through it using a Socratic approach. Ask me questions, one at a time, and wait for my response before continuing.**

> *ChatGPT:*
> *When you choose one option over another, what—specifically—do you think you're giving up? (Answer in one line.)*
>
> **You said:**
> I give up the potential benefit of the thing I didn't choose
>
> ***ChatGPT said:***
> *Exactly. That's the essence of opportunity cost: the value of the* ***next-best alternative*** *you didn't choose.*
> *Let me push you one step deeper:*
> *If you had to measure that cost, would you do it in* ***money****,* ***time****, or* ***something else****?*
>
> **You said:**
> It could be all of those
>
> ***ChatGPT said:***
> *Right—opportunity cost can be measured in money, time, energy, or even missed experiences.*
> *Here's my next question:*

If you decide to spend tonight writing for two hours instead of relaxing with friends, what is the real opportunity cost of writing?

You said:
I have two: building my connection with friends and giving up fun

ChatGPT said:
Good—you've identified ***non-monetary opportunity costs****: relationships and enjoyment.*
Now let me turn it around: if you instead choose to spend the evening with friends, what would be the opportunity cost of not writing?

You said:
Getting the work done, so adding pressure and feeling guilty

ChatGPT said:
Exactly. So in either choice, you're trading one set of benefits for another. Here's the next step: when you look at both sets of costs and benefits—fun with friends vs. reduced pressure from writing—what do you think should guide your decision?

You said:
If I've turned down my friends a couple of times, keeping the connection would be more important if I knew I could still get my work submitted on time.

ChatGPT said:
That's a solid reasoning step—you're weighing ***context*** *(recent choices) and* ***deadlines*** *(submission on time).*
Here's the next question: in that situation, how would you clearly define the opportunity cost of choosing friends over writing?

You said:
The damage of submitting my work either late or less polished

ChatGPT said:
Yes—and notice how specific that is: late or less polished work is the concrete cost of your choice.
Next question: if the deadline is still comfortably far away, how does that change the size of the opportunity cost?
(Dialog continues.)

Choosing a Technique

This section covered two approaches to learning new knowledge. The first uses the Ask & Refine style of interaction; the second uses Socratic dialog. Use the approach that is most comfortable for you.

Choose Ask & Refine when:

- You want a fast, structured answer with minimal overhead.
- You already have a basic grasp of the topic and want to fill in gaps or clarify details.
- You're working under time pressure or embedding this into a larger task like a report, meeting, or presentation.

A Socratic dialog may be more useful when:

- You are facing a complex, unfamiliar, or abstract topic, you may not know or have a cursory knowledge of, such as systems thinking, organizational behavior, or ethical strategy.
- You're unsure what you don't know and need to uncover or evaluate assumptions before you can build understanding.
- You're preparing for a strategic decision or defending your ideas and want to sharpen your reasoning by exploring alternatives and implications.

And remember, you can switch between the two approaches at any time.

Build Your Concept Learning and Practical Skills

Learn and expand practical skills through guided practice and feedback.

Concept learning is understanding principles, while *skill building* is developing the ability to perform tasks. Concept learning is best acquired through a series of guided questioning, using either Guided Q&A or Socratic-style dialog or a combination of the two. You may have to go through several sessions, ending each by asking ChatGPT to give you an assignment you can think about and pick up in the next session, or feedback on what you've mastered and what you can work on further.

Skill-building requires practice and feedback to achieve steady improvement to perform a task with increasing proficiency. With ChatGPT, you can develop practical skills more efficiently by working through step-by-step guidance, targeted exercises, and immediate, personalized feedback. Each interaction can include clear instructions, structured practice tasks, and suggestions to help you refine your approach and build confidence as you go.

Prompt Template for Skill-Building

Here is a simple prompt template for skill building:

I'd like to learn how to [specific skill]. Provide clear, step-by-step guidance, give me a practice task, and offer constructive feedback when I complete it.

Example Prompts For Building Specific Skills

Here are examples of prompts to build common skills that are good to master as they are useful in all walks of life.

- Writing Skills
- Project Management Skills
- Presentation Skills

Writing Skills

- **I want to improve my skill in writing effective email subject lines that grab potential customers. Give me guidelines, assign me a practice email scenario, and provide detailed feedback to improve my result.**
- **Help me learn how to structure a persuasive email to a client. Please also provide three additional practice prompts for related skills.**

Project Management Skills

> **Help me build my skill in creating clear project timelines. Explain the steps involved, ask me to draft a timeline for launching a simple marketing campaign, and critique my output.**

Presentation Skills

> **I'd like to learn how to introduce a business presentation effectively. Give me guidelines, ask me to draft a one-minute introduction for a sales pitch, and offer feedback to make it stronger.**

ChatGPT provides step-by-step instructions for the skill you're learning. It will then offer you an actionable practice task. Once you complete the task, ChatGPT will deliver personalized feedback highlighting strengths and areas for improvement.

Continuous Practice Loops Foster Growth and Mastery

To *master* a skill, you need a lot of practice. The initial learning curve is steep, and it becomes easier the more you practice the skill until it ultimately becomes intuitive. Continuous practice loops are developing skills through continuous practice and feedback to achieve increasing levels of proficiency and mastery.

Sample Prompt Template and Prompt

Here is a prompt template that initiates a continuous practice skill-building session:

> **I want to learn [skill].**
>
> - **Please start by briefly explaining what this skill involves and why it's valuable. Then guide me through continuous practice with short, interactive exercises. After each one:**
> - **Provide feedback on my answer,**
> - **Explain what I did well or where I could improve,**
> - **Then give me a new exercise.**

Keep going until I say stop.

Example prompt:

- **I want to learn how to write concise, persuasive emails for business.**
- **Start by explaining the key elements. Then give me continuous practice. After each one, provide feedback, tell me what to improve, and give me another.**
- **Continue until I say stop.**

Example of a Skill-Building Dialog

Imagine your goal is to become a better writer, and you want to learn how to improve poorly written sentences. Following is a sample prompt:

I want to learn how to simplify and improve poorly written sentences.

Please start by explaining what makes a sentence poorly written. Then guide me through short, interactive exercises. After each one:

- **Give me a flawed sentence,**
- **Let me revise it,**
- **Then give feedback on my revision,**
- **And present another sentence to improve.**

Continue until I say stop.

This prompt produced the following dialog:

ChatGPT:
Poorly written sentences are often too long, vague, or use passive voice. They may rely on weak verbs, redundant phrases, or confusing structure. Your goal is to rewrite each one to be clearer, more direct, and more readable.

Let's begin!

Exercise 1:

"The report was written by the manager in order to make clear what the expectations of the team were supposed to be."
Try rewriting this sentence to make it simpler and more direct.

(User replies with their revised sentence)

ChatGPT:
Great attempt! Here's what you did well...
Here's what could be improved...
A possible version: "The manager wrote the report to clarify team expectations."
Let's try another.

"Due to the fact that the project deadline was approaching quickly, the team members were asked to work extra hours in order to complete their assignments on time."
Your turn.

(Dialog continues until you say Stop.)

Takeaways for Chapter 9

This chapter shows how you can use conversational techniques to acquire new knowledge and strengthen your skills. ChatGPT provides structured explanations, guided practice, and feedback that adapts to your pace. Through active engagement, ChatGPT helps you turn information into increasing levels of expertise.

Key points:

1. **Ask & Refine** provides clear explanations with interactive checks and is most helpful for Skill-Building.and diving deeper to acquire and build knowledge on a topic.
2. **Socratic dialog** fosters deeper insight through guided questioning and is most helpful for higher level reasoning such as ambiguous topics, principles and concepts.

3. **Skill-building exercises** allow practice and immediate feedback.
4. **Continuous practice loops** help you improve until a skill feels natural.
5. Learning is most effective when you **connect** new knowledge to existing experience or apply it to a current assignment.

PART 4

Serious Writing and High-Impact Documents

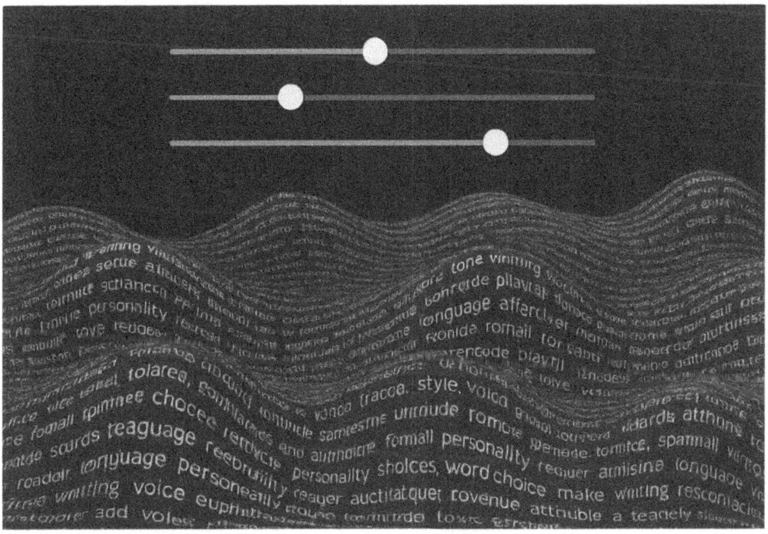

This section is for people who write documents that go beyond quick communications. Whether you're creating policies, white papers, proposals, articles, or books, you need documents that are clear, well-planned, and polished.

You'll learn how to use context files to share your vision and keep ChatGPT focused. We'll cover style guides that streamline repetitive work. You'll explore brainstorming, outlining, drafting, and generating diagrams and illustrations. We'll also look at tone and voice so your drafts sound like you.

CHAPTER 10

Creating High-Impact Documents

To think is easy. To act is difficult. But to act as one thinks is the most difficult.

—Johann Wolfgang von Goethe

In Chapters 3 and 4, we focused on using ChatGPT to quickly create informational documents. These everyday documents are one-time communications like notes, invitations, or announcements. They're typically built with a single, well-structured prompt that includes purpose, audience, tone, style, length, format, and key points. With that in place, you can often get a clean draft that only needs light editing.

These documents are used every day, but they are not what you need for important or formal communications.

Crafted Documents

For important, sensitive, and nuanced communication, you need another kind of writing I call *crafted documents*. These are high-impact pieces that need to be carefully shaped, considered and reviewed for clarity and accuracy. They stick around longer, reflect your voice and vision, have potential for greater impact, and benefit when edited more intentionally.

Unlike everyday documents, which emphasize speed and clarity with minimal effort, crafted documents demand clarity and impact that comes with high-quality thinking, strategic organization, and strong writing. They reflect your ideas and priorities, so you must guide ChatGPT to align with your goals for the communication and audience

Crafted documents are often longer and more complex than simple communications, but they can be concise and brief. A short mission statement or opinion piece require depth and precision that can withstand scrutiny or unintended interpretation. Other crafted pieces, like books, reports, proposals, articles, or strategic analyses, tend to be more extensive and structured with multiple sections and cross-references.

This chapter, and the three that follow, will guide you through designing and writing these high-impact documents. The core techniques are similar to what you've already seen. What changes is the *level of thought, revision*, and alignment with your personal or professional *voice.*

Regardless of length, crafted documents involve multiple iterations and a strategic vision designed to deliver long-term value. It's also important to detect misleading or misinformation that sounds accurate but is incomplete, biased, or incorrect.

Crafted Documents Workflow

Like any serious writing task, there's no single way to create a crafted document. Some writers begin with a detailed outline, while others prefer to dive straight into drafting. Some revise obsessively, fine-tuning every word; others write more loosely and edit later. No matter what workflow you prefer, ChatGPT can *assist* with much of the writing task while still allowing your unique voice and style to come through. Remember that *you* are responsible for the content and end result – not ChatGPT.

As you gain experience working with ChatGPT regularly, you'll develop a rhythm that fits both your working style and the demands of each project. Over time, based on your interactions, ChatGPT will adapt to you as well. If you keep your account active, the more you use ChatGPT it can begin to recognize your tone, preferences, and the kind of output you expect. It learns from the level of specificity you use in your prompts and interactions.

Here are some of the ways you can use ChatGPT to support your writing process:

1. Research – After Summarize background material and surface relevant, credible sources.
2. Brainstorming – Generate ideas, supporting arguments, and alternative perspectives.

3. Assumption Testing – Reveal and challenge hidden assumptions or weak logic.
4. Critical Review – Pressure-test your arguments and conclusions.
5. Outlining – Turn a loose list of ideas into a structured outline.
6. Drafting – Expand bullet points or outlines into full, well-written prose in your voice.
7. Proofreading – Catch grammar issues, typos, and awkward phrasing.

Working with a Word Processor

At the time of this writing, ChatGPT, Gemini, and Claude do not have strong file management or document editing capabilities. You'll often find yourself copying text back and forth between your browser and ChatGPT.

ChatGPT can export Word files. Gemini cannot export Word files directly, but you can ask for a plain text file to be displayed that you can copy and paste into Word. Claude can produce formatted text called "artifacts." These are displayed in a side panel and, when copied and pasted into Word, retain most of the formatting.

Working on Longer Documents

If you are creating a long document, you may find it helpful to open two Word windows. Use one document (Word1) for drafting and editing. When you're satisfied with a section, paste it into the second document (Word2) to assemble your final document. This keeps your polished version clean and organized.

Work in Sections

It's tempting to paste a large outline into ChatGPT and ask for a full draft. But this rarely produces high-quality results. When the task exceeds ChatGPT's memory limits, the writing becomes vague, repetitive, or generic.

To get better results, work in manageable sections. You can paste your outline into ChatGPT and ask how much it can handle without losing quality. The answer will vary depending on which version of ChatGPT you're using. With a paid GPT-5 account, you have a larger context window, so you can paste longer documents.

Use Meta Commands to Work Faster

A *meta command* is a short label you add to a prompt to signal a specific task. It acts like shorthand, so you don't need to repeat detailed instructions every time. Meta commands save time, reduce typing, and help you work more consistently. For example

- Rev: Asks ChatGPT to review and rewrite a paragraph for clarity, tone, grammar, and engagement. You can define Rev.
- Fix: Asks for grammar and spelling correction only, without changing the tone or structure. You can define Fix.

These are not built-in commands; you can define meta commands however you like. Just tell ChatGPT what each one means and how it should respond. For instance:

- **When I type 'Rev:' before a paragraph, review and rewrite it for clarity, tone, grammar, and engagement.**
- **Treat 'Fix:' as a command to correct grammar and spelling only.**

You can also ask ChatGPT to suggest other useful meta commands based on your workflow.

Using Context Files

Yogi Berra, the legendary baseball catcher, once said, "If you don't know where you are going, you'll end up someplace else." If he had been a writer, he might have said, "If you don't know what you're writing, you'll end up writing something else." And he'd be right!

To get accurate and consistent results from ChatGPT, you need to provide *context*—background information that frames your request.

This can include project goals, writing style, audience, structure, or any other detail that shapes the task.

In Chapter 7, we discussed *condensed context files* that summarize the key points of a chat so you can paste them into a new session and continue seamlessly.

Context files also serve another purpose in writing. They help ChatGPT maintain focus and consistency across longer projects. This type of file is usually one page and works like a project brief. You can create it in Word and either paste it directly into the chat or upload it at the start of your session.

A context file uses plain language. The format is flexible. As long as it is clear, ChatGPT will process it effectively. Following is an example of a context file for working with ChatGPT.

Context File: Working With ChatGPT

Purpose:
Create an eBook that explains how ChatGPT can help business professionals save time and effort—both in routine tasks and in strategic or creative assignments.

Target Audience:
Business professionals at all levels, including those working in large corporations, small businesses, nonprofits, and freelance roles such as consultants, contractors, and content creators.

Goals:
To equip readers with practical skills and foundational knowledge for using ChatGPT effectively. Readers should learn how to streamline their work, improve efficiency, support strategic thinking, and enhance their professional influence. The book should help readers build both hands-on capabilities and a deeper understanding of how to think with AI.

(*Continued*)

Style and Tone:
Authoritative but friendly—professional, respectful, and conversational. The tone should build trust while making the content approachable and engaging.

Meta Commands (for this project):

- Rev: Review and rewrite for clarity, tone, engagement, smoothness, and flow.
- Proof: Correct grammar and spelling only—no stylistic changes.
- Acc: Check the passage for accuracy and rewrite as needed.

Prompt for Pasting in Your Context File

The easiest way to give ChatGPT context is to paste in the context file at the beginning of the session. A sample prompt is:

> **Use the following as context for all prompts in this session. This is for the project called [Project Name]. Please retain and apply it throughout. [Paste context here]**

If you prefer to *upload* a context file, it's best to use a name that clearly indicates its contents, such as context file for book project.docx. This helps ChatGPT identify the file and apply it appropriately without needing to open it.

Using Style Guides for Consistency

A *style guide* refers to a short set of instructions that tells ChatGPT what to include and in what order. It has a specific meaning in an AI context. Think of it as a template that defines structure for the document. You decide the elements—such as headings, bullet points, or standard wording—and ChatGPT fills them in for you. If you're writing *sections* such as case studies, project summaries, bios, or FAQ entries, a style guide can save time and keep the format of repeated sections consistent

Although you may be familiar with the term "style" used by Word, this should not be confused with a *style guide* as we are using it here. ChatGPT does not format text. You can do that in Word or another word processing program.

You can create a style guide to provide the raw information for each new section, or you can ask ChatGPT to draw on its knowledge base to create a style guide for you Either way, it formats the content according to the style guide so that every *section* looks the same and follows the same rules.

A style guide does not need to be long or complex. A few clear steps are enough. For example, you might tell ChatGPT:

- **Start with a one-sentence summary.**
- **Add three bullet points with key details.**
- **End with a short takeaway.**

Once you create a style guide, you can reuse it as often as needed to produce clear, uniform content quickly. If you are using a context file you can include style guide directly or you can paste it in separately.

When you use a style guide, you can supply the raw facts, and ChatGPT will shape them using the guide. Or you can ask ChatGPT to generate the ideas and use the guide to format the response. For example, you might ask ChatGPT to generate 10 techniques for team performance and format them according to your style guide.

Example of a Style Guide

Imagine you are creating a set of brief biographies of famous contributors to computing. For example, Ada Lovelace who wrote the first computer program in 1843. Charles Babbage who built the first computer in 1833, and Steve Jobs who, with Steve Wozniak, developed the first Apple computer in 1976.

There are potentially many such biographies, and we want them all to have the same format, so we create a simple style guide. For example:

Style Guide: Short Biographical Profile
Each entry should follow this format:

- Name: Full name of the person
- Occupation: Job or professional role
- Notable Achievements: 2–3 bullet points highlighting key accomplishments
- Personal Fact: A short, humanizing, or unusual detail
- Tone: Neutral, informative, and friendly
- Length: Keep the full entry under 150 words

Example Prompt Using the Style Guide

The simplest way to use the style guide is to paste it into a prompt like this:

- **Use the style guide below to write a biographical profile of Ada Lovelace.**
- **[Insert style guide here]**

This prompt results in the following bio:

Name: Augusta Ada King, Countess of Lovelace
Occupation: Mathematician and Writer
Notable Achievements:

- First to recognize that Charles Babbage's Analytical Engine could be programmed.
- Authored what is widely considered the first algorithm intended for machine processing.
    - Pioneered the concept of a general-purpose computing machine over 100 years before computers existed.

Personal Fact:
Ada was the daughter of the famous poet Lord Byron but had no relationship with him after infancy; her mother encouraged a strict focus on science and mathematics instead.

Each bio will follow the same format following the style guide, resulting in a consistent document.

Case Study: Backyard Birds

We'll explore the use of context files and style guides with this case study.

Imagine you've been hired by the local Bird Watchers Club to create a short eBook (5,000–8,000 words) to sell on their website. The club has two primary goals:

1. Raise funds to support their activities.
2. Attract new members by sparking local interest in birdwatching.

There's just one catch: you're not a bird expert. The closest you've come to ornithology was the weekend you reluctantly bird-sat your aunt's parakeet. Still, you accept the challenge.

Define The Context File

Your first step is to define the project by creating a context file in Word. The example here is moderately detailed—you can simplify it if you prefer. A well-written context file like this can also double as a briefing document for stakeholders at the start of a project.

Context File: Backyard Birds
Project Description
A beginner-friendly guide to backyard birdwatching, designed to educate and inspire readers while promoting the local Bird Watchers Club.

(*Continued*)

Goals:

- Generate revenue for the club through eBook sales.
- Encourage new members to join.
- Provide useful, engaging content for local bird enthusiasts.

Target Audience

- Local homeowners and nature lovers
- Casual birdwatchers and families
- Anyone curious about attracting birds to their yard

Tone and Style

- Conversational and engaging – like chatting with a friendly birdwatcher
- Easy to understand – no dense scientific terms
- Encouraging – birdwatching should feel fun and accessible

Create the Style Guide

The eBook will include a section featuring descriptions of backyard bird species. To ensure each entry follows the same structure, tone, and depth of information, you'll use a style guide. This will help ChatGPT deliver consistent results and make editing easier.

Our style guide provides entry titles and a picture. Since style guides cannot control page layout, we'll have to reformat the information once generated, but it will be consistent for each bird species.

Style Guide for Backyard Birds
Bird Name

- Use the common name of the bird as the main heading. Write it in Title Case. Example: Northern Cardinal

Scientific Name

- Place the scientific name immediately below the common name in parentheses. Italicize it.
  Example: (*Cardinalis)*

Did You Know?

- Start with a quirky or surprising fact to capture interest. Keep it to 1–2 short sentences. This should be fun, memorable, and something unique about the bird.

What It Looks Like

- Describe the bird's size, shape, colors, and any distinct features. Use casual, colorful language that helps the reader picture it easily.

What It Sounds Like

- Describe the bird's call or song using sound words or fun comparisons. Example: "It sounds like a laser gun from an old video game."

Where T to Find It

- Explain where the bird is typically found, especially in a local backyard or park setting. Mention regions, climate preferences, or nesting habits if relevant.

What It Likes to Eat

- List typical foods in the wild and what people can offer (e.g., specific seeds, fruits, or feeders). Mention any feeding behaviors that are fun or noticeable.

How to Invite It Over

- Give practical tips for attracting the bird—types of feeders, water features, native plants, or nesting boxes. Keep tone helpful and encouraging.

Picture This!

- Generate a square, photo-realistic illustration (1024 × 1024 pixels, .jpg format). The style should be lifelike but visually appealing—ideal for an eBook aimed at beginners.

(*Continues*)

Tone & Style

- Use conversational, positive language throughout.
- Avoid technical jargon—keep it light and fun.
- Write in short, vivid paragraphs that are easy to read on screen.
- Humor and personality are welcome, but don't let it overwhelm the facts.

With the style guide, a lot of the writing will be done. Since ChatGPT has all the information about birds in its knowledge base, you can ask it to recommend species and then create the entries following the style guide rules. It is best to produce the entries one at a time.

Example: Generating an Entry

In this example, we'll use the style guide to have ChatGPT generate an entry for the Blue Jay. The output below is presented *unformatted* output produced by ChatGPT:

Blue Jay
(Cyanocitta cristata)

Did You Know?
Blue Jays are expert mimics! They can imitate the calls of hawks to scare off other birds—or just for fun.

What It Looks Like
With brilliant blue feathers, a black collar, and a jaunty crest on top, the Blue Jay is one of the flashiest birds in the backyard. Its wings and tail are streaked with white and black, making it easy to spot even from a distance.

What It Sounds Like
Loud and proud! Its call ranges from a sharp "jay jay!" to odd squeaky whistles and clicks. Sometimes it sounds like it's auditioning for a robot role in a sci-fi movie.

Where to Find It
Blue Jays love wooded areas and suburban yards with tall trees. You'll spot them in parks and neighborhoods across the eastern and central U.S.

What It Likes to Eat
They enjoy peanuts, sunflower seeds, corn, and berries. They'll even visit feeders with suet or mealworms.

How to Invite It Over
Offer a platform feeder or scatter peanuts in the shell. They like open yards with big trees—and they'll remember your yard if the food's good!

Picture This!

Formatted Example: Robin Redbreast

In this example, the output was generated by ChatGPT using the same style guide used in the unformatted example, then pasted into Word and formatted. Here is the how the original unformatted ChatGPT output looks after being formatted.

Robin Redbreast

(Turdus migrators)

Did You Know?

Robins are one of the first birds to sing at dawn—so much so that they're sometimes called the "alarm clocks of spring."

What It Looks Like

With a bright orange-red chest, gray back, and white eye ring, the robin is easy to recognize. It often tilts its head while listening for worms—an iconic backyard sight.

What It Sounds Like

Their song is cheerful and rich, like a flutist warming up on a sunny morning: "cheerily, cheer-up, cheerily, cheer-up."

Where to Find It

Common throughout North America, robins are found in yards, parks, gardens, and fields—especially in the early morning.

What It Likes to Eat

Robins love earthworms, fruits, and berries. They'll snack on mealworms and chopped fruit if offered near the ground.

How to Invite It Over

Provide a low platform feeder or scatter mealworms and soft fruit. A nearby birdbath is a big bonus—they love to splash!

Takeaways for Chapter 10

Crafted documents differ from everyday documents in scope, depth, and purpose. While everyday documents are fast and functional, crafted documents, such as reports, proposals, policies, and books, require more structure, clarity of purpose, and editorial care.

1. When drafting a crafted document, consider:
    - Define the project with a context file.
    - Consider using a style guide if you have repeated elements.
    - Generate draft text in sections using ChatGPT.
    - Edit and format in Word or other word processing app.
2. Context files and style guides help ChatGPT stay aligned with your goals, tone, audience, and structure.
3. Meta commands like Rev: or Fix: allow you to speed up editing and maintain consistency without retyping instructions. Remember, you can name and define your own meta commands.
4. The case study, Backyard Birds project, shows how to use context files and style guides in practice. Note the output is unformatted.
5. The case study, Robin Redbreast, demonstrates the next step, taking the unformatted output produced by ChatGPT and edit it in another app to format the finished product.

CHAPTER 11

Brainstorming

The best way to have a good idea is to have lots of ideas.

—Linus Pauling

The term brainstorming may be familiar to you as a technique used by groups or teams to generate as many ideas as possible. In this chapter we are using the term brainstorming in a different context.

When you undertake a writing project, *brainstorming* techniques can help you gain insights you use to shape your ideas and build a clear, coherent flow for what you want to communicate. In addition to this chapter, you will find related techniques in Chapter 5 (Build a Document Interactively), Chapter 6 (all techniques, particularly Prepare to Defend Your Ideas), and Chapter 8 (Brainstorm a Strategy). ChatGPT's ability to analyze and challenge your arguments is one of its most useful capabilities.

By engaging in a dynamic exchange of exploring questions, and possibilities, you develop a deeper and more focused view of your topic and uncover new angles you might have missed. ChatGPT can draw on its vast base of knowledge and respond to you in natural language.

Even if you know your subject well, exploring it from multiple angles clarifies your thinking and uncovers ideas and perspectives you might not have considered. It's easy to rule out some ideas you don't think will be accepted. Or, you might have strong ideas based on past experience that you may not have questioned in a while. Information-overload and time constraints don't make it easy to assess the value of changes in the field.

Through brainstorming, you can:

1. Expand your knowledge.
2. Consider multiple perspectives.
3. Generate new ideas.
4. Identify gaps or blind spots in your thinking.
5. Create a high-level outline summarizing content and flow.

Brainstorming with ChatGPT is energizing because it helps clarify your vision and construct a roadmap to guide your writing and presentations.

Start with Your Own Ideas

Brainstorming requires an open mind. One of the risks of brainstorming with AI is that you will accept its initial ideas before you have fully considered other perspectives.

Research shows that brainstorming on your own *before* using AI leads to more creative, focused results. It's like outlining: starting with a few bullet points is far more effective than starting from scratch. Even when your initial ideas are rough and disorganized, you begin building a mental framework that helps you process AI responses more clearly and judge their quality more critically.

A few minutes of solo thinking, or a short chat with a colleague, can make your AI session faster, sharper, and more useful.

High-Level Outline

The goal of brainstorming with ChatGPT is usually to create a high-level outline that serves as a roadmap for your writing or presentation. The high-level outline is typically two levels deep: *main ideas* and *supporting points*. It lays out the structure, content, and flow. A two-level outline is easy to work with. Depending on your preference, you can have ChatGPT expand it and generate draft text, or write it yourself.

If the subject matter is too complex or nuanced to be fully laid out in the high-level outline, you can expand it into a more detailed outline to elaborate. Expansion is most effective after the initial brainstorming process, once you have a complete picture of how you want to structure the topic.

Case Study: Time Management

In this chapter, we'll brainstorm a high-level outline for a handout on time management. This handout could be used for a workshop, as a stand-alone document, or even as the foundation for a series of blog posts.

The purpose of this case study is to demonstrate the kinds of output you can get by brainstorming. Like writing, how you approach brainstorming depends on your own style, needs, and preferences.

We'll use two interaction styles:

1. The *Ask & Refine* style, where you create prompts asking ChatGPT questions and follow-up to refine the initial response.
2. The *Guided Q&A* style, where ChatGPT asks you questions and steers the interactive conversation based on your answers.

Both approaches work well; combining them works even better. Here we're going to brainstorm a high-level outline for Time Management. In the next chapter, we will use the outline to generate text.

Time Management

You know from painful experience that juggling a busy schedule is tough, and during meetings, you've noticed a pattern: many people are overwhelmed, working inefficiently, and constantly stressed as they struggle to stay on top of everything. Determined to help, you decide to create a short workshop on time management techniques.

You recognize that a brief presentation is not likely to change anyone's behavior. Your participants need a practical handout they can use to test out different time management strategies and decide which work best for them.

Excited by the opportunity, you also realize you've just added a big project to your already packed calendar. And let's be honest, you could use a little time management support yourself. That's when you turn to ChatGPT for brainstorming help in designing and creating your time-saving guide.

Planning the Handout

Since the target audience consists of busy professionals, both the workshop and handout must be short, practical, and engaging. Time is already a scarce resource, so you need to capture and hold participants' attention with content that is valuable immediately actionable, memorable and enjoyable.

The time management techniques you present should resonate immediately, making their relevance clear. They must be easy to use and presented with a fresh, compelling perspective.

Start with Context

You will get the best results from a brainstorming session if you provide ChatGPT with context that helps it focus and avoids generic responses. You can create a context file, as discussed in Chapter 10. If that is more than you want for a brainstorming session, you can just explain your situation to ChatGPT using a prompt. In either case, the goal is to help ChatGPT identify what is most relevant to you.

Here is a sample context file you can upload or paste in at the beginning of the brainstorming session:

Context File: Time Management

Purpose:
This document helps business professionals, consultants, and content creators optimize their time to produce high-quality work efficiently. It balances short-term tasks with long-term objectives and provides adaptable strategies for different professional needs.

Target Audience:

- Business professionals
- Consultants and freelancers
- Content creators

Tone and Style:

- Conversational, direct, and concise
- Friendly and upbeat
- Practical and actionable advice
- Engaging and easy to follow

Use a prompt to notify ChatGPT that you are pasting in the context file:

Here is a context file. Please use it for the rest of this session.

[Paste context file here.]

Beginning the Dialog

You may want to start the session by asking ChatGPT questions directly. Here are some questions you can try to help ground your thinking:

- **What are effective ways to present time management concepts?**
- **Where do professionals typically struggle with time management?**
- **What common mistakes waste time?**
- **What techniques help solve these problems?**
- **How can we organize these techniques for easy access and experimentation?**

When you get the initial response, ask follow- up questions to get more detail on anything promising.

Structured Dialog

Alternatively, you can have ChatGPT ask you structured questions, one at a time. Respond with any ideas that occur to you without worrying about completeness or flow. ChatGPT will organize and summarize your ideas and use then to guide the conversation. Prompt it to challenge you so you can think about objections and refine your approach.

Example prompt*:*

I want to create a time management workshop but I'm not sure where to start. Please ask me questions one at a time to help clarify the content, structure, and goals. Analyze my responses to guide the conversation, and feel free to challenge my assumptions or suggest alternatives where helpful. Help me figure out what to include in a productivity guide. Ask me questions to explore my goals, audience, and priorities.

Choosing an Angle

Angles in this context are the various perspectives for approaching your topic. For example, one angle might be to look at the psychological factors that contribute to procrastination. Another might be to look at how people set priorities.

We'll begin exploring perspectives with a prompt asking a broad question that gives us a high-level view of possible angles, along with how you would like the output formatted.

> **I'm developing a handout to teach Time Management techniques to busy professionals. What are different ways I could organize the content overall? Please consider multiple perspectives or organizing principles. Present the results in a table with one row per approach. Column 1: a simple, friendly name for each approach. Column 2: a concise description of the organizing method. Column 3: your evaluation of how well each approach might resonate with, and deliver value to my target audience.**

Requesting output as a table makes it easy to compare different approaches. ChatGPT used this prompt to generate output in a table with eight approaches to consider.

Approaches to time Management

Approach	Definition	Evaluation for Busy Professionals
Problem-Solution	Presents common time management struggles and provides techniques to solve them.	Highly effective—directly addresses pain points and provides clear, actionable solutions.
Step-by-Step System	Introduces a structured method, guiding readers through progressive time management skills.	Useful but may feel rigid; busy professionals may prefer flexible techniques over a fixed system.
Quick Wins First	Starts with easy, high-impact techniques before moving to deeper strategies.	Very engaging—delivers immediate value, keeping readers motivated.
Skill-Based Sections	Groups techniques by key time management skills (e.g., prioritization, focus, delegation).	Practical—lets readers identify areas for improvement, but may require effort to apply systematically.
Daily Routine Focus	Organizes techniques around different parts of the workday (morning, midday, evening).	Helpful for those looking to structure their day but may not fit every professional's schedule.

Approaches to time Management

Approach	Definition	Evaluation for Busy Professionals
Use-Case Driven	Tailors strategies to specific roles or work-styles (e.g., freelancers, executives, teams).	Personalized and relevant but requires effort to navigate for those seeking general advice.
Efficiency vs. Effectiveness	Divides techniques into those that boost efficiency (speed) vs. effectiveness (quality).	Insightful but may need clear guidance to help readers apply both concepts effectively.
Common Mistakes to Fix	Highlights major time-wasting habits and how to correct them.	Engaging and relatable—easy to digest and apply, making it great for professionals.

Each approach presented in the output resulting from the prompt has merit. Given the heavy schedules and short attention spans of our audience, we think we're more likely to get good results by combining a discussion of typical behaviors that lead to inefficiency, with "quick wins," and step-by-step instructions. That would enable participants to identify problematic behavior patterns that create inefficiency and provide them with concrete solutions to try.

Combining Approaches

You're not limited to choosing just one approach. You can ask ChatGPT to help combine several of them into a hybrid structure. We'll do this using a structured dialog where ChatGPT asks questions to guide the process.

Here's a prompt you can use:

> **I see value in several different approaches and would like your help combining them into a format that's engaging, works well in a short handout, and resonates with my audience. Please ask me targeted questions, one at a time, to help shape a hybrid structure that draws from problem-solving, quick wins, step-by-step guidance, and common mistakes. If you think my answers could be improved, feel free to challenge or refine them. Once you have enough input, please present your recommended structure in a table, including the key elements, brief definitions, and any comments you think are useful.**

This prompt led to the dialog that follows. It is long but produced useful results:

ChatGPT:

Great approach! Let's start shaping the best structure for your handout.

First Question:

Your audience is busy professionals who need quick, practical solutions. Would you prefer to start with Quick Wins to immediately engage them, or begin with Common Mistakes to make them aware of what's holding them back?

Each has a different psychological effect:

Quick Wins first hooks readers with immediate benefits.

Common Mistakes first creates awareness and urgency before providing solutions.

Which feels more effective for your audience? Or do you see value in another approach?

You:

I would prefer to begin with common mistakes. I would like to organize the common mistakes into 3-4 categories that are intuitive to my audience. Rather than calling these "mistakes" I think it would be more upbeat to refer to them as Time Thieves: opportunities to use time more efficiently and save effort. When we define each of them, we can present a quick win as the first technique for each opportunity.

ChatGPT:

That's a strong approach—starting with "opportunities" instead of "mistakes" keeps it positive while still engaging readers. Organizing them into 3-4 intuitive categories will make the content easier to navigate.

Next Question:

What broad categories feel most natural to your audience? Based on common struggles, some possibilities include:

- *Overcommitment & Prioritization – Struggling to say no, unclear priorities.*

- *Distractions & Interruptions – Constant emails, meetings, and task-switching.*
- *Inefficient Workflows – Poor planning, redundant effort, and reactive work.*
- *Procrastination & Motivation – Avoiding difficult tasks, inconsistent progress.*

Do these categories resonate, or would you adjust them? If so, how?

You:

I like these a lot. I am not sure if they are in the best order. It feels to me that procrastination should be higher in the list. Perhaps swap 3 and 4. I am also a bit uncertain about motivation. It could be seen as accusatory (e.g., 'you are not motivated'). Are you OK with leaving it out even though we lose the symmetry of two terms per category?

ChatGPT:

Great instincts. Swapping Procrastination & Motivation with Inefficient Workflows makes sense—procrastination is a major barrier that should be addressed earlier.

I agree that "motivation" can feel accusatory or misplaced. We can drop it and simply call the category Procrastination—it's a common challenge that doesn't need an extra term for balance. The categories don't have to be perfectly symmetrical as long as they feel natural and intuitive.

Here's the revised order:

1. *Overcommitment & Prioritization*
2. *Distractions & Interruptions*
3. *Procrastination*
4. *Inefficient Workflows*

Does this feel right to you? Would you like to tweak the wording or structure further?

You:

I like the structure. I think we can tweak the wording so each category (challenge) is cast in a positive light. I would suggest: 1. Managing overcommitment & priorities, 2. Minimizing distraction & interruptions, 3. Beating procrastination, and 4. Creating efficient workflows. These are quick thoughts so if you have a punchier idea I am open to it.

ChatGPT:

Your wording is strong and keeps the focus positive. I have a few refinements for even more clarity and punch:

1. *Managing Priorities & Commitments – Emphasizes control rather than struggle.*
2. *Reducing Distractions & Interruptions – Keeps "minimizing" but sounds more active.*
3. *Overcoming Procrastination – "Beating" is good, but "overcoming" feels more constructive.*
4. *Designing Efficient Workflows – "Creating" is solid, but "designing" suggests intentionality.*

These retain your intent while making the phrasing smoother and more engaging. Do these work for you?

You:

Yes. Your changes are fine.

ChatGPT:

Great! Now that we have the core structure, let's move to the next step.

Next Question:

For each of these four categories, we'll introduce a Quick Win—a simple, high-impact technique that immediately helps the reader. These should be:

- *Easy to implement right away*
- *Practical and relevant to most professionals*
- *A natural lead-in to deeper strategies*

Here are some possible Quick Wins for each category. Let me know if any stand out, or if you'd like to adjust them:

1. *Managing Priorities & Commitments → The "Not Now" List – A simple way to separate immediate priorities from distractions.*
2. *Reducing Distractions & Interruptions → The "Do Not Disturb" Hour – A daily block of protected, interruption-free work time.*

3. *Overcoming Procrastination → The 5-Minute Start – Commit to working on a task for just five minutes to overcome inertia.*
4. *Designing Efficient Workflows → Batching Similar Tasks – Grouping similar tasks (emails, calls, planning) to save time and mental energy.*

Do these Quick Wins align with your vision, or would you like to tweak or swap any?

You:

These are OK. I am not familiar with Not Now but know about ABCD and the Eisenhower Matrix. Which would you think works best for 1.

ChatGPT:

The Eisenhower Matrix is a great tool, but it might feel too structured for a quick win. The ABCD method is simpler but still requires categorization.

The "Not Now" List is a lightweight version of these—anything important but not urgent goes on a separate list, preventing distractions while keeping valuable tasks visible. However, if you prefer a more established method, I'd suggest:

For Managing Priorities & Commitments: The ABCD Method – Rank tasks as A (urgent/important), B (important/not urgent), C (low-priority), or D (delegate). Simple and flexible.

Would you like to use this, or do you prefer something else?

You:

I think ABCD would be good. It also addresses the problem of to-do lists that get so large they become overwhelming.

ChatGPT:

Great choice! The ABCD Method is intuitive, easy to apply, and helps manage overwhelming to-do lists.

Next Step:

Now that we've set the Challenges & Quick Wins, I'll compile everything into a structured table for clarity. Here's what we have.

The requested structure in the output table that follows is solid but incomplete for use as a handout in the format in a high-level outline that is easy to read and absorb.

Challenges and quick wins

Opportunity	Definition	Quick Win
Manage Priorities	Preventing overcommitment and focusing on what truly matters.	The ABCD Method – Rank tasks as A (urgent/important), B (important/not urgent), C (low-priority), or D (delegate).
Avoid Distractions	Creating focus by minimizing unnecessary disruptions and interruptions.	The "Do Not Disturb" Hour – A daily block of protected, interruption-free work time.
Overcome Procrastination	Tackling avoidance and building momentum on important tasks.	The 5-Minute Start – Commit to working on a task for just five minutes to overcome inertia.
Design Efficient Workflows	Streamlining work processes to maximize efficiency and reduce wasted effort.	Batching Similar Tasks – Grouping related tasks (emails, calls, planning) to save time and mental energy.

Developing a High-Level Outline

We will use the structure presented in the table output as a starting point for a handout. The handout needs an introduction, a conclusion, and multiple techniques under each opportunity.

Since the goal is to keep the handout brief, adding two additional techniques to each category brings the total to 12, a practical and manageable number for busy readers.

I asked ChatGPT to suggest five additional techniques for each category. To keep this chapter concise, I've omitted the full lists and selected two strong additions per category.

With this expanded set of ideas, I used ChatGPT to help shape a high-level outline. After a few iterations, we arrived at a well-structured format that builds on the original concept and meets the goals of the handout.

Writing a Description

I asked ChatGPT to write a brief blurb describing the handout that could be shared with participants. Reading it, you can see that ChatGPT has developed a clear model of the content and flow:

ChatGPT:

This handout is structured to be practical, engaging, and easy to follow. It is built around four key opportunities for improving time management. Each opportunity highlights a quick win to get results immediately and introduces two additional techniques to deepen your skills.

Every technique includes a simple explanation, step-by-step guidance, and common mistakes to avoid, so you can apply it with confidence. The goal is to help you experiment with different approaches and find the ones that fit your unique work style.

The High-Level Outline

ChatGPT created a high-level outline based on the session. The outline was produced using Prompt 4 (Create an Outline or Framework) in the output below:

1. Introduction
    - Time – the scarce resource
    - Why time management matters
    - The four opportunities
    - Find the techniques that work for you (including Quick Wins)
2. Manage Priorities
    - Quick Win: The ABCD Method
    - The Eisenhower Matrix
    - The 80/20 Rule (Pareto Principle)
3. Limit Distractions
    - Quick Win: Turning Off Notifications
    - The Pomodoro Technique
    - Scheduled Email & Message Checks
4. Overcome Procrastination
    - Quick Win: The 5-Minute Start
    - Reward Yourself
    - Divide & Conquer

5. Streamline Workflow
   - Quick Win: The Two-Minute Rule
   - Templates & Checklists
   - The "One-Touch" Rule
6. Conclusion

We are satisfied with this high-level outline, but additional prompts could help make it even better. The only way to know is to try them out.

Additional Brainstorming Prompts

Here are eight brainstorming prompts that you can use. Try them out to see how ChatGPT responds:

Bird's Eye View

The bird's eye view gives you high-level insights to your topic.

This prompt is useful when you want to start thinking about your overall document strategy and define its scope and goals. This will help you:

- Get a broad sense of possibilities before narrowing focus.
- Establish key themes or questions to explore.
- Identify constraints or specific requirements upfront.

Prompt:

I'm planning to develop a long-form document on [topic]. What are some different angles I should consider, along with key themes and possible ways to structure the content? Please present your suggestions clearly and concisely, and feel free to include a table if it helps organize the options.

ChatGPT will suggest big-picture ideas, potential themes, and structural directions to help you shape your project.

Targeted Questions

ChatGPT will ask you targeted questions and construct an outline or story from your responses. This technique is useful when you need to:

- Clarify your approach before outlining.
- Explore different perspectives to find the best angle.
- Generate fresh ideas and avoid writer's block.

Prompt:

I want to brainstorm ideas for a [type of document] on [topic]. Please ask me targeted questions, one at a time, to explore different angles, key themes, and structural options. Guide the process step by step, adjusting based on my responses. When you have enough information, create a [high-level outline | summary | case study | other output].

ChatGPT will guide you through a structured brainstorming session, ensuring that your ideas develop logically while keeping the process dynamic and interactive. This prompt works best when you provide context information up front, to guide ChatGPT's questions.

Explore Broad Perspectives

This prompt is useful when you need fresh ideas, diverse viewpoints, or a deeper understanding of your topic. It will help you:

- Discover new ways to approach your topic.
- Find unique angles that differentiate your work.
- Explore different ways your audience might interpret the subject.

Prompt:

Give me a wide range of perspectives on [topic]. How might different audiences—such as professionals, beginners, skeptics, or decision-makers—approach or interpret this? Highlight key concerns, priorities, or framing differences for each group.

ChatGPT will generate a variety of perspectives, themes, and angles to spark your creativity.

Create an Outline or Framework

This is the prompt used to create the high-level outline in this chapter. Use this prompt if you want to take your brainstormed ideas and turn them into a structured outline.

- Sort key themes into logical sections.
- Create an outline that makes drafting easier.
- Decide what belongs in your document and what doesn't.

Prompt:

Based on our previous discussion, can you organize these themes into a structured outline with section headings?

ChatGPT will generate a structured outline or list of themes to help you organize your thoughts.

Refine Your Ideas Before You Start Writing

If you want to strengthen your outline before drafting, this prompt can:

- Ensure your ideas and arguments flow logically.
- Identify gaps, weak spots, or missing elements.
- Solidify your structure so the writing phase goes more smoothly.

Paste your outline directly into the chat—either as a numbered list, bulleted structure, or section headings. Then use the following prompt:

Does this structure fully cover [topic]? What's missing, unclear, or out of sequence?

ChatGPT will review your outline, identify any missing elements, suggest improvements to flow and logic, and recommend ways to strengthen your structure before you begin drafting.

Challenge Your Assumptions

If you want to make your writing more nuanced and persuasive, exploring alternative perspectives can help you strengthen your arguments and avoid confirmation bias that you might not even be aware of.

Prompt:

What are the strongest counterarguments to my main points, and how might I address them?

ChatGPT will generate relevant counterpoints and suggest thoughtful rebuttals, helping you refine your position and anticipate objections.

Gather Research and Supporting Arguments

If you need more depth, evidence, or real-world support, AI can help you surface examples and strengthen your case.

Prompt:

Provide evidence, case studies, or historical examples that support the argument in [section].

ChatGPT will suggest examples, data points, or research findings that add depth and validation to your argument. This is one area where you should *check the validity of any evidence you are quoting* to make sure it is from a legitimate, recognized source (with a cited reference), vetted for accuracy, fact-checked or otherwise verified - and not a hallucination or convincing misinformation.

Test Your Clarity and Flow

Use this prompt to ensure your content is clear, concise, and logically organized.

Prompt:

- **Please read the following text and produce a brief summary that outlines its main point, supporting arguments, and logical structure. The goal is to help me quickly evaluate whether the passage is clear, well-organized, and coherent. Use bullet points or a short paragraph if appropriate. Do not rewrite the content—just distill it.**
- **Text to analyze: [Paste your text here]**

ChatGPT will distill your content into a concise summary, helping you evaluate clarity, structure, and logical progression that is easy to absorb at a glance.

Takeaways for Chapter 11

Brainstorming with ChatGPT is an efficient way to shape your ideas, explore different perspectives, and build a strong structure before writing. This chapter demonstrates how dynamic interaction, both by asking questions and responding to ChatGPT's prompts, can help uncover insights, identify gaps, and organize content effectively. Using a case study on time management, the chapter illustrates how brainstorming can lead to a practical, high-impact outline for a workshop handout. The chapter also introduces a set of reusable brainstorming prompts.

1. Brainstorming clarifies thinking and strengthens structure. Even a brief session can surface new angles and lead to a more coherent document.
2. You will often get the best results if you do some brainstorming yourself before engaging with the AI process. Preparatory work prepares you to gain more insight.
3. A high-level outline is the goal of brainstorming. It serves as a roadmap. It defines your structure, context, and flow concisely and guides the generation of full text.

4. Context matters. Uploading a context file or including key background information helps ChatGPT stay aligned with your goals.
5. You can brainstorm by asking ChatGPT direct questions or prompting it to ask you structured questions. You can combine both styles in a session.
6. You don't need to choose just one approach. If multiple organizing frameworks show promise, ask ChatGPT to help you combine them into a hybrid structure.
7. Let ChatGPT challenge your assumptions, help prioritize content, and refine your arguments.
8. Prompts like "Give me a wide range of perspectives" or "What are the strongest counterarguments?" can unlock new insights and deepen your content.
9. Whenever you will be presenting research or other data to others, it's important to ask for citations, vet the information and be on the lookout for hallucinations or misleading, doctored or content taken out of context that can look convincing.

CHAPTER 12

Generating Text

If you do enough planning before you start to write,
there's no way you can have writer's block.

—R.L. Stine

In the previous chapter, we developed a high-level outline for our time management handout. Now it's time to turn that outline into usable content. This is where your role as a writer becomes essential. You can have ChatGPT develop the initial draft or start with your own writing and use ChatGPT to edit.

Start With an Outline

Earlier, we generated text from prompts, often starting with bullet points. The process here is similar, but you will usually begin with an outline. You can work from a high-level outline or expand it for more detailed content and flow.

The level of detail depends on how much control you want. A quick method is to take a high-level outline and annotate it with bullet points that capture the key ideas you want to cover. This both expands your content and defines the flow.

The writing process works best *section by section*. Avoid pasting a long outline into a single prompt and asking ChatGPT to generate text all at once. That almost always produces weak results.

How Large a Section Should You Work On?

For best results, keep each section focused and manageable. If the section is too long, ChatGPT may lose focus, oversimplify, or fall back on generic language. If it's too short, it may not provide enough context to produce continuity.

Here are a few guidelines:

- Topic-based sections work well (e.g., one heading from your outline).
- If a section has multiple bullet points, you can include those as supporting ideas in the prompt.
- If you're not sure, start small. You can always expand, add detail, or ask for a rewrite.

This strategy helps ChatGPT stay focused and ensures that each part of your document reflects your intent. It creates a workflow that makes it easy to edit individual sections while you are focused on them.

If you manually edit the high-level outline, upload or paste the revised version to ChatGPT. If it has access to the entire outline, it will use it to ensure continuity, reduce redundancy, and create smoother transitions between sections. In some of the prompts that follow, it is suggested that you paste in a copy of the output line. You only need to do this if ChatGPT has lost access to it.

The Time Management Outline

Here is a copy of the outline we brainstormed in the last chapter:

1. Introduction
    - Time – the scarce resource
    - Why time management matters
    - The four opportunities
    - Find the techniques that work for you (including Quick Wins)
2. Manage Priorities
    - Quick Win: The ABCD Method
    - The Eisenhower Matrix
    - The 80/20 Rule (Pareto Principle)
3. Limit Distractions
    - Quick Win: Turning Off Notifications
    - The Pomodoro Technique
    - Scheduled Email & Message Checks

4. Overcome Procrastination
   - Quick Win: The 5-Minute Start
   - Reward Yourself
   - Divide & Conquer
5. Streamline Workflow
   - Quick Win: The Two-Minute Rule
   - Templates & Checklists
   - The "One-Touch" Rule
6. Conclusion

Next, we'll move to creating context followed by content, working section by section, in manageable amounts of text.

Creating Context

Before using the outline to guide text generation, it is best to establish context for ChatGPT, so the text generated is relevant, focused, and reflects the tone and style you want. We'll start by pasting in the context file we used for brainstorming we did in Chapter 10 when we began work on the Time Management project

Generating the Introduction

We'll begin text generation with the Introduction section generated in the original, unedited outline, using a minimalist prompt to generate a 200-word introduction:

Write a 200-word introduction to the Time Management handout.

Follow the outline:

1. Introduction

Time – the scarce resource

Why time management matters

The four opportunities

Find the techniques that work for you (including Quick Wins)

Here is the text that the prompt above produced:

Introduction

Time is the one resource you can't make more of. Money, energy, ideas—you can usually find ways to replenish them. But time only moves forward, and once it's gone, it's gone. That's why managing your time isn't about squeezing more into your day. It's about spending your time on what matters most.

Whether you're juggling client demands, team meetings, or creative work, time pressure can erode focus, increase stress, and limit your impact. The good news is that time management isn't about rigid systems. It's about making smarter, more deliberate choices.

This guide focuses on four key opportunities: avoiding overcommitment, managing distractions, improving prioritization, and developing consistent workflows. These aren't theoretical ideas—they're concrete, flexible techniques you can try, adapt, and combine.

You don't need to use every technique in this guide. Start with one or two that match your current challenges. Look for quick wins—simple strategies that make an immediate difference. Then build from there. The goal isn't perfection; it's progress.

What follows is a practical, easy-to-use set of ideas that help you take back control of your time and focus your energy where it counts.

This is a typical ChatGPT draft. It hits all the desired points, but it's boring and uninspired. It's not likely to capture our audience or generate a lot of enthusiasm.

There are a number of indications that you can use to recognize generic AI writing. The initial paragraph screams AI wrote this. It can be improved just by cutting extra words:

"Time is the one resource you can't make more of. That's why managing your time is about spending your time on what matters most."

Note that a variant of the structure "X is not about Y, it's about Z," appears five times in the text. This is a common AI sentence structure that is frequently generated.

Also note the use of what is commonly called "em dashes"—these are grammatically correct – routinely used by ChatGPT but not used frequently in human writing (shorter dashes with a space on either side.)

Editing the Outline

We can improve the quality of the generated text by making the outline more specific. We'll do this by adding bullet points to the outline, so ChatGPT will follow our flow and include the key points we want to emphasize. We'll also add some instructions to improve the tone. Here is an enhanced prompt:

Write an engaging introduction for the time management handout using the outline below. Use a friendly, conversational and metaphorical tone and generate about 200 words:

1. Introduction

- **Time – the scarce resource**
- **Why time management matters**
- **The four time thieves [explain each in a sentence using friendly, metaphorical language]**
- **Overcommitment**
- **Distraction**
- **Poor Prioritization**
- **Inefficient Workflow**
- **Find the techniques that work for you (including Quick Wins)**

Each time thief has three techniques to improve time management below it.

- **The first is a quick win that is easy to try out.**
- **The other two require more thought but may be more powerful**

Here is the text that resulted from this prompt:

> ## Introduction
>
> Time is the one resource you can't stockpile, stretch, or get back once it's gone. It slips through meetings, emails, and multitasking faster than we realize—and that's where better time management comes in.
>
> This handout is your practical guide to spotting and beating four of the most common "time thieves"—those sneaky patterns that quietly steal your day:
>
> Overcommitment—saying yes to everything until your to-do list overflows
>
> Distraction—getting pulled away by pings, pop-ups, and "just one quick thing"
>
> Poor Prioritization—working hard… but not always on what matters most
>
> Inefficient Workflow—bouncing from one thing to another without finishing anything
>
> You won't find lectures here—just smart, simple techniques you can try. Each time thief comes with three strategies to help you take control of your time. The first is a Quick Win—an easy fix you can try immediately. The other two go a bit deeper and may take more effort—but the payoff is worth it.
>
> Use this guide like a toolbox. Try what fits. Leave what doesn't. The goal is progress, not perfection—and maybe even a little more time to breathe.

This text is more engaging and closer to the introduction we want. It does have a lot of em dashes, which can be replaced by other punctuation. Let's try again, but alter the tone to make it less casual using this prompt:

Please generate another version. This time make it more formal in tone.

This prompt generated the text that follows:

Introduction

Time is one of our most limited and valuable resources. Unlike money or materials, it cannot be saved, borrowed, or replaced—once it is spent, it is gone. That's why effective time management is essential for professionals who want to maintain focus, reduce stress, and achieve meaningful results.

This handout introduces four common challenges that undermine productivity—what we refer to here as "time thieves":

Overcommitment—taking on too much, leading to overload and burnout

Distraction—frequent interruptions that fragment attention and reduce efficiency

Poor Prioritization—focusing on less important tasks at the expense of strategic goals

Task Switching—constantly shifting between tasks, which increases mental fatigue and delays completion

For each of these time thieves, you'll find three practical techniques to help you regain control. The first is a Quick Win—a simple, low-effort strategy you can apply immediately. The remaining two are more involved, offering deeper and potentially more lasting improvements.

This guide is designed to be flexible. Explore the techniques, apply what resonates, and adapt them to your needs. The ultimate objective is to work more intentionally—protecting your time so you can focus on what truly matters.

As you work with text generation prompts, you'll develop a style and tone that fits your target audience. If you wish, you could replace em dashes with traditional dashes in your final Word edit of the document.

In Chapter 14, you will find a comprehensive list of styles and tones, suggestions for combining them, and an explanation of how to upload a writing sample that ChatGPT can use as a model to generate text in your voice.

Generating Content Sections

With the Handout Introduction complete, we're ready to generate the rest of the content.

We'll start with two time thieves:

1. Managing Priorities, and
2. Overcommitment

You may have noticed that *we're not working through the outline in order*. Because we have four sections with the same structure, it's faster to generate the similar pieces in parallel and assemble them in Word at the same time, then continue with the next sections.

We'll use two different techniques:

1. For the Introduction to Managing Priorities section, we will have ChatGPT generate full text based on a list of bullet points pasted into a prompt.
2. For the Introduction to Overcommitment section, we will write a draft and have ChatGPT edit it.

Content Generation: Next Two Text Sections Using Two Techniques

Next, we will take on another two sections to demonstrate two different techniques for generating text.

Content Generation: Managing Priorities

ChatCPT Converts Bullet List to Text

The high-level outline on Managing Priorities lacks details, so we'll provide ChatGPT with a list of bullet points. When pasted into the prompt, ChatGPT will follow the sequence and expand on each point. The bullet points contain an instruction to "include a case study," which ChatGPT will interpret and use to generate a short illustrative example.

A simple prompt that will convert the bullet points into full text is:

Please use the bullet points that follow to generate full text:

- **This section is called "Managing Priorities."**
- **Why poor prioritization is a time thief: important work is often delayed or overlooked.**
- **Leads to missed deadlines or rushed work on tasks that matter most.**
- **Increases stress and decision fatigue from constant reprioritization.**
- **Include a case study or example of someone who struggles to complete critical tasks due to poor prioritization.**
- **Clarify key distinctions that contribute to prioritization problems:**
- **Confusing high-value tasks with low-value activity**
- **Mistaking being busy for being effective**
- **Treating urgency and importance as the same**
- **If you're not clear about your priorities:**
    - **It becomes harder to say no because nothing is clearly defined as most important**
    - **You default to reactive mode, sacrificing strategy and long-term results**

The *advantage* of this approach is that you are in control of the content and flow. You can get to a draft quickly and feel confident that it conforms to your intent. It's a compromise between allowing ChatGPT to decide on the details and putting in the effort to write a polished draft.

Here is the text output, ready for you to edit:

> **Managing Priorities**
>
> Poor prioritization is one of the most common and costly time thieves. When you haven't clearly defined what matters most, it's easy to get pulled into work that feels urgent but adds little value. Important tasks are postponed, rushed, or even forgotten altogether. The result? Missed deadlines, lower quality output, and a growing sense of stress and frustration.
>
> Constantly shifting priorities can lead to decision fatigue—where the energy spent choosing what to focus on leaves you too drained to do the work well. And without clear priorities, it becomes harder to say no. Everything seems equally important, so everything gets a piece of your attention—even if it doesn't deserve it.
>
> Many people struggle because they confuse activity with effectiveness. They stay busy, but not productive. Others treat urgency and importance as the same, jumping at the next alert or request instead of planning around what truly moves their goals forward.
>
> Consider a consultant who spends most of the week answering low-priority emails and fine-tuning minor client updates—only to realize on Friday that a key proposal hasn't been started. This kind of misalignment is avoidable. Managing priorities helps you regain control of your time and focus on what will have the greatest impact.

Next, we'll turn to the next section.

Content Generation: Overcommitment

ChatGPT Edits Draft Text Provided

To create the section on overcommitment, we will use a different approach. Instead of starting with bullet points, we will draft the text ourselves and then ask ChatGPT to edit it. This takes more effort but gives you greater control over the final result.

If choosing the right words slows you down, you may value ChatGPT's role as an editor. You can write quickly, produce a rough draft, and let

ChatGPT smooth the text. The result is a polished version that usually needs only a light edit to meet your standards.

You may find that ChatGPT is a terrific editor. It can smooth and clarify your text without changing your focus or flow. You can request an initial edit and then ask for further refinements by saying things like:

- **"Make it more engaging"**
- **"Make it more concise"**
- **"Make it read more smoothly"**
- **"Improve clarity"**
- **"Make it more persuasive"**
- **"Make the tone more formal | informal | conversational |..."**

Using *Meta Commands* for Editing

In Chapter 10, we explained how to create meta commands like *rev*: which instructs ChatGPT to edit text according to your specifications. You don't have to use it, but it's a real time saver if you are doing a lot of editing.

In this example, we'll start with a rather poorly written explanation of overcommitment – one of the four "time thieves," – and ask ChatGPT to improve it.

Here is the initial rough draft based on the meta command we provided:

Overcommitment

If you take on every task that comes your way. If you can't say "no" there is a real chance that you will become overcommitted. Let's face it – there are only so many hours in a day. And you have only so much energy. You have to use them wisely.

If you are overcommitted, you will be rushed. Instead of giving your all to a job you will do a slapdash job just to get it done. This will hurt your reputation and the value people place on your work. Also you won't have time to focus on improving your skills and knowledge so you don't make yourself more valuable.

For all these reasons and more you need to avoid over commitment.

To clean up this rather messy explanation, we'll use the following prompt:

Please review and improve the text that follows. Correct any errors and make it sound smooth and professional. If you feel I have left out anything important, expand the text to include it.

Here is the edited text generated by ChatGPT based on the prompt:

Overcommitment

If you accept every task or request that comes your way and struggle to say "no," there's a significant risk you'll become overcommitted. Let's face it—there are only so many hours in the day, and your energy is limited. It's essential to use your time and resources wisely.

When you're overcommitted, you end up rushed and overwhelmed. Instead of giving your best effort, you produce hurried work simply to meet deadlines. Over time, this can damage your reputation and diminish others' perception of your professional abilities. Even worse, your own satisfaction and confidence may decline as the quality of your work may decline.

Additionally, constant overcommitment leaves little or no room to develop new skills, deepen your expertise, or reflect strategically on your priorities. Without opportunities for growth, your value to your team, clients, or organization is likely to stagnate or even decline.

For all these reasons, it's critical to set clear boundaries and prioritize tasks intentionally. Protect your time, focus your energy, and avoid the trap of overcommitment.

This initial edit improved the rough draft, but it's not good enough. We'll ask ChatGPT to edit the improved text, changing some of the words and shifting the tone:

Please rewrite and improve the text that follows without changing the overall flow or message. Avoid redundant use of the word decline. The tone should be friendly and persuasive but remain authoritative. Here is the text: [paste text here].

This prompt resulted in the third iteration of the text:

> **Overcommitment**
>
> If you accept every task or request that comes your way and struggle to say "no," you risk becoming overcommitted. There are only so many hours in the day, and your energy is limited. To succeed, you must use both wisely.
>
> When you take on too much, you end up rushed and overwhelmed. Instead of delivering your best, you produce hurried work just to meet deadlines. Over time, this can harm your reputation and weaken others' confidence in your abilities. Just as important, your own sense of satisfaction may suffer as the quality of your work slips.
>
> Chronic overcommitment also crowds out time for growth. You lose the chance to build new skills, deepen expertise, or step back and think strategically. Without this space, your long-term contribution to your team, clients, or organization can level off or even diminish.
>
> To avoid these risks, set clear boundaries and make deliberate choices about where to invest your effort. Protect your time, direct your energy, and keep your commitments aligned with your highest priorities.

This is improved and requires only minor edits to polish the section.

Content Generation: Using a Style Guide for Techniques

The next section we'll tackle are Techniques.

We want our handout to include 12 Time Management techniques (three for each time thief), making it an ideal candidate for a style guide. *Each technique is designed to stand alone, allowing it to function as a quick reference.* To keep readers engaged, each entry will include a visually appealing image and a short, relatable story to bring the technique to life.

ChatGPT has access to a wide range of established time management methods, eliminating the need for in-depth research on your part. However, it's good practice to run the generated content through a *plagiarism checker* to ensure originality. If any section appears too close to published material, you can either revise it or add a reference, for a professsional product.

Creating The Style Guide

Here is the *style guide* we will use to generate each of the 12 sections, so that they are all in the same format.

> Style Guide: Time Management Techniques
> Each entry should include:
>
> - Name of the technique
> - One-sentence tagline explaining what it does
> - Brief paragraph describing how it works
> - Origin story—who created it or how it became popular
> - Amusing, relatable example of someone using the technique successfully
> - Step-by-step bullet list for how to implement it
> - Automatically generate a humorous 3D-style illustration that visually captures the technique's concept (highest possible resolution, square format)

Pasting in the Style Guide

We will paste the style guide into a prompt. We can then reference it in subsequent prompts to create our Time Management techniques. Here is the prompt:

- **Use the following as the style guide for a series of Time Management techniques I will ask you to generate. Apply it strictly when I reference it in a prompt.**
- **[Paste style guide here]**

We'll use the style guide to produce an entry for the Pomodoro technique:

Please use the style guide Time Management Techniques to write a draft text section on the Pomodoro Technique.

Running this prompt produces the technique. As ChatGPT does not have the capability to specify page layout, it was necessary to do a bit of reformatting after the text was pasted into Word. Here is a formatted and lightly edited version, which will be repeated in format for each of the 12 techniques.

The Pomodoro Technique

The Pomodoro Technique helps you stay focused by breaking work into short, timed intervals—typically 25 minutes of concentrated effort followed by a short break. This rhythm keeps your mind fresh and reduces burnout while improving your ability to estimate time and resist distractions.

Pomodoro is the Italian word for "tomato." The technique was invented by Francesco Cirillo in the late 1980s. The name Pomodoro came from the tomato-shaped kitchen timer he used as a university student. What started as a personal strategy to improve study habits has since become a global productivity classic.

How Carlos Got His Proposal Done

Meet Carlos, a freelance designer who couldn't finish a client proposal without checking email, scrolling his phone, and rearranging his desk twice. Then he discovered the Pomodoro Technique. With a kitchen timer ticking beside him, he committed to just 25 minutes of focused work. By the third Pomodoro, he'd finished the proposal—and realized he hadn't even opened Instagram. Victory!

How to Use the Pomodoro Technique

1. Choose a task to work on.
2. Set a timer for 25 minutes.
3. Work on the task—no interruptions!
4. When the timer rings, take a 5-minute break.
5. After four Pomodoros, take a 5 minute break.
6. Repeat as needed.

Content Generation: Expanding Sections

The outline does not provide any detail for the Conclusion Section, so we'll ask ChatGPT to expand that section. This is a quick way to *add depth* while still giving you the chance to review and edit before moving on to full draft text.

You can use this same process on any part of a high-level outline. Expanding one section at a time allows you to create a detailed outline, refine it with bullet points, and improve flow before drafting.

Expand the Outline to Draft Text

The best practice is to work in three steps:

1. Ask ChatGPT to expand the section.
2. Review and edit the expanded outline, adding bullet points to strengthen content and flow.
3. In a separate prompt, generate the draft text.

Trying to combine outline expansion and text generation in a single prompt often produces weaker results.

Here is a prompt template for expanding a section of the outline:

- **Expand the [section name] of my outline into a detailed outline. Use clear bullet points that add structure and content. Do not write full text yet.**
- **Here is my outline:**
- **[Paste outline here]**

Creating Content: Expand Outline to Create Conclusion

Running the prompt above to expand the Conclusion section of the outline produced this detailed outline for the section, ready for review and editing:

Conclusion

Restate the core theme: time is a scarce resource that must be managed deliberately

Summarize the key areas covered in the handout:

Managing priorities

Limiting distractions

Overcoming procrastination

Streamlining workflow

Reinforce the idea of "quick wins" as easy entry points for lasting change

Emphasize that no single method fits everyone—encourage readers to experiment and adapt

Highlight the long-term payoff: greater focus, productivity, and satisfaction in both work and personal life

Suggest practical next steps:

Choose one technique to try today

Build habits gradually by adding more techniques over time

Reflect regularly on what is working and adjust as needed

Close with a motivating call to action that positions time management as a lifelong skill worth refining

Generating the Text from Enhanced Outline

Here is a prompt template for generating the draft text:

- **Write draft text for the [section name] of my book based on the outline below. Do not include the outline itself in the response.**
- **[Paste the expanded and edited outline section here]**

Running this prompt with the expanded outline (lightly edited text) produced the following:

Conclusion

Time is the one resource you cannot replace, so managing it deliberately is essential. This handout has shown you practical ways to take control of your time by managing priorities, limiting distractions, overcoming procrastination, and streamlining workflow.

Quick wins give you an easy starting point. A small change—such as turning off notifications or starting a task for just five minutes—can create momentum and lead to lasting improvement. The key is to build confidence with small steps and expand from there.

No single method works for everyone. Your challenge is to test, adapt, and discover the mix of techniques that fit your work and personal style. The payoff is worth the effort: more focus, higher productivity, and greater satisfaction in both professional and personal life.

To move forward, pick one technique and apply it today. As it becomes a habit, add another, and continue to reflect on what helps you most. Adjust as needed to keep your system effective.

Time management is not a one-time fix. It is a lifelong skill that grows stronger with practice. Start small, stay consistent, and make your time work for you.

ChatGPT Assists - But You are Responsible for the End Product

This chapter introduced several techniques for generating text. There is no single best method. The right one is the approach that helps you produce clear writing with the least wasted effort.

AI today does a solid job with nonfiction, but *it cannot replace the judgment and intent of a human writer.* ChatGPT works best as a tool that reduces (not replaces) effort. It can produce structured drafts and smooth rough text, but **you** are responsible for the final product and should always review and edit the result

Not every document deserves the same level of care. A crafted piece, such as an article published under your name, must reflect your ideas and intent. That means editing carefully so key nuances are preserved. By contrast, a project summary may only need to be accurate, well-structured, and clear. In either case, ChatGPT can save you time while still leaving control in your hands.

Most drafts it generates will not be perfect, but with guidance, especially through context files, it can deliver text that fits your tone and style and requires only light revision. In Chapter 14, we will look more closely at how to guide ChatGPT with tone, style, and writing samples so it reflects your personal voice more faithfully.

Finally, remember that using AI in writing is not free of *controversy.* In everyday business communication, it may not be an issue, but the risk of passing along misleading or misinformation is real and often hard to detect. In producing any document for distribution or publication, disclosure and citing sources is the *ethical standard.* Using AI as an assistant *strengthens* your work; handing over authorship *undermines* your credibility. Use ChatGPT to reduce effort and refine your writing but keep authorship and responsibility firmly your own.

Takeaways for Chapter 12

This chapter guides you through ways to use ChatGPT to generate text, turning a high-level outline into well-crafted, structured content. It emphasizes the importance of balancing AI support with human judgment and offers strategies for both generating and refining text. It suggests working in sections to keep ChatGPT focused and using context and style guides to create structure and continuity.

1. Start with a high-level outline, then expand or annotate it with key bullet points to guide ChatGPT's output.
2. Work in small sections (150–300 words) to keep results focused and high quality.
3. Use a context file or include clear instructions in your prompt, including tone, structure, and specific ideas you want covered. Ask for sources as needed.
4. Edit and iterate: ask for revisions, review your edits, and rephrase manually to fit your objectives and style.
5. Revised outlines should be pasted in or uploaded to maintain continuity and structure across sections.
6. Style guides help maintain consistency in format and tone, especially for repeated elements like techniques or case studies.
7. You can ask ChatGPT to create case studies and examples to make your text more relatable.
8. Use ChatGPT for visual support too, generating illustrations when appropriate.
9. Try different techniques to find what works for you.
10. Always maintain authorship responsibility for the documents you produce.

CHAPTER 13

Creating Visual Content

Pictures can communicate ideas in seconds that might take pages of text to explain.

—Dan Roam, author of The Back of the Napkin

A document that consists only of text can be dull or even intimidating to some readers. Visuals are great for telling a story—a very powerful communication technique. Well-designed visuals can you clarify your message, making it easier to quickly grasp and absorb, and stay engaged. A picture, as we are often told, is worth a thousand words.

Creating good visuals takes work, talent and knowledge about how to quickly and precisely convey a message that is immediately clear to everyone. If you are an artist, great! But if you're not, and you want to include visuals, you will have to look elsewhere for your graphics.

Some visuals are largely decorative, while others help you communicate your message. A well-created *flowchart* or *diagram* can communicate a process more effectively than words alone. An *infographic* encourages your readers to explore key ideas. If your document is electronic, you can even consider including *audio* or *video*. Or you may want to incorporate a variety of ways to present the same message to a diverse audience, which is increasingly favoring different modes of communication.

Of course, if you have the budget or talent, you can create graphics outside ChatGPT, and that is often the easiest approach. That being said, you can use AI to produce decorative illustrations and diagrams. While AI can produce a wide range of visuals, it can be a challenge to get exactly what you want.

Decorative illustrations add personality and engage your audience. AI can create stunning graphics that work as cover art, blog post headers, chapter leaders, and illustrations that you can use for text and presentations.

Diagrams communicate information that can make complex ideas clear by communicating flow, process, and structure in a way that can be easily be absorbed.

How to Create AI Graphics

The process of creating AI graphics is a lot like the process you use to create text. You write a prompt that explains what you want and instruct the AI platform to generate a result. The more explicit the prompt, the more likely you are to get something you like.

But just as you have to edit ChatGPT's generated text if you want a really well-written document, you may also need to edit the graphics that are produced. Editing graphics and videos is harder than editing text. You may not need to edit decorative illustrations since you have a lot of flexibility, but diagrams need to be accurate.

Why Use AI for Visuals?

Wouldn't it be great to have access to a graphic designer who worked at lightning speed, was available 24/7, and was really inexpensive? That's the claim generative AI offers, for example:

- Speedy results enabled by AI tools can whip up visuals in seconds.
- Budget—friendly graphics that don't look like common stock photos.
- Ease of use—even beginners can create impressive graphics with a little practice and patience.
- Diverse styles—from photorealism to funky abstract art—giving your illustrations a fresh, exciting look that can appeal to a diverse audience

But let's not sugarcoat things. AI is far from perfect. Getting what you want may be frustrating or more work than you're willing to undertake. Sometimes AI delivers surprises you didn't ask for.

Here are some common hurdles:

- **Unpredictable results**. You might ask for a "modern office," and the AI gives you a space with a chair floating in mid-air. Or you ask for a picture of a horse, and it comes back with five legs. Remember, ChatGPT and other generative AI platforms don't understand how the world really works or experience it in the way humans do.
- **Inconsistent results**. Put the same prompt in twice, and you will get two different images. That can be a plus, but it can also be problematic if continuity of style and content is important. For example, imagine you want to show a business team in different situations. You want the same people and the same furniture and office décor in each image. That kind of continuity is easy for human graphic artists, but a problem for most AI platforms.
- **Technical limitations**. Need print-ready graphics? Some tools don't make it easy to adjust resolution or DPI (i.e., Dots Per Inch), information you need to know for the visuals you create to render properly. You may need to upscale the results using special software if your goal is commercial publishing.
- **Learning curve**. Prompts for illustrations are more difficult to craft than prompts for generating text, although the platforms are getting better at interpreting your intent.

Using DALL-E for Illustrations

DALL·E is a *text-to-image platform* developed by OpenAI—the same organization behind ChatGPT. It generates images based on natural language prompts.

The latest version of DALL·E is integrated directly into ChatGPT, making it easier than ever to brainstorm a design concept with ChatGPT, refine your prompt, and generate images—all in one place. This integration means you often don't need to use DALL·E separately, which is a real benefit.

That said, communication between ChatGPT and DALL·E isn't always perfect. The good news is that DALL·E has improved significantly and now allows you to make visual edits directly within ChatGPT, so you can refine and regenerate images as needed.

In most cases, you'll get decent results with a simple, well-written prompt. But if you want greater control over the final image, you may have better results by explicitly specifying any of the elements below in your prompt or as follow up:

1. **Main subject**: Describe the primary focus of the image (e.g., "a red apple on a dark brown,wooden dining room tabl').
2. **Background**: Specify the background details (e.g., "a sunset over a calm sea").
3. **Colors**: Mention specific colors you want in the image (e.g., "a vibrant orange sunset").
4. **Lighting**: Describe the lighting conditions (e.g., "soft, diffused lighting").
5. **Style**: Indicate the artistic style (e.g., "in the style of Van Gogh" or "realistic"). Here are some examples of ways you can convey styles to spark your imagination and ideas.
   - You can generate images in the style of well-known, deceased artists (like Van Gogh or Monet).
   - To reduce the risk of triggering content filters, use phrasing like "inspired by" or describe specific visual characteristics of the style (e.g., "thick brushstrokes and swirling skies reminiscent of Van Gogh").
6. **Perspective**: Specify the viewpoint or angle (e.g., "bird's-eye view" or "close-up").
7. **Additional elements**: Include any extra details or objects (e.g., "flying cars" or "neon signs").
8. **Emotions or mood**: Describe the desired setting you're trying to convey (e.g., "a serene and peaceful scene").
9. **Size and aspect ratio**: It's important to know what your options are so that your images will render in the best way possible so that they render properly. Choose from available sizes like 1024 × 1024, 1792

× 1024, and 1024 × 1792. ChatGPT can help you choose what you want or need.

There is an almost infinite list of styles that you can specify. To help you get started, here are 10 styles you can use with ChatGPT:

1. **Realistic**: Creating lifelike images with accurate details and proportions.
2. **Surreal**: Blending reality with fantasy elements for a dreamlike effect.
3. **Impressionist**: Mimicking the brushstrokes and color palettes of Impressionist painters like Monet.
4. **Abstract**: Focusing on shapes, colors, and forms rather than realistic depictions.
5. **Cartoon**: Generating images with a playful, animated style.
6. **Vintage**: Emulating the look of old photographs or retro illustrations.
7. **Cyberpunk**: Combining futuristic and dystopian elements with neon colors and high-tech aesthetics.
8. **Minimalist**: Using simple, clean lines and limited color palettes.
9. **Fantasy**: Creating magical and mythical scenes with fantastical creatures and landscapes.
10. **Pop art**: Inspired by the bold colors and graphic styles of artists like Andy Warhol.

This is not a complete list, so here's a chance to get creative! You can even ask for an Anime style! You have a lot of flexibility. An important thing to bear in mind is that DALL-E will *not* produce images that depict violence or hate. For example, if your prompt request is for:

A 3D rendering of a two-story house, shaped like a shoe, pink with laces set in a childlike garden on a sunny day at a resolution of 1792x1024 DALL-E.

More than one output may be generated by ChatGPT using this same prompt. Following are two generated outputs resulting from the same prompt, submitted twice.

Output #1

A 3D rendering of a two-story house, shaped like a shoe, pink with laces set in a childlike garden on a sunny day at a resolution of 1792x1024 DALL-E.

Output #2

How can this happen?

The first thing we notice is that the two images created by ChatGPT using the same prompt reflect different perspectives – which could happen by simply asking ChatGPT to "Try again" after the first image was created.

Notice that in the second drawing, both the swing set and the slide are partly outside the fence. This is an example of the *unexpected violations of reality* that are common in AI images. This happens because ChatGPT does not experience reality in the same way humans do. Without specific direction, it would not know where backyard items belong.

You can access DALL-E through ChatGPT. Just tell ChatGPT what you want in an image, and it will pass the prompt on to DALL-E. ChatGPT will check the prompt for completeness and will add additional information if it determines that DALL-E needs a more specific prompt than you provided.

You can also access a simple version through Microsoft's Bing Image Creator.

Canva

Canva is a *versatile graphic design platform* that allows you to create a wide range of visual content. Its user-friendly interface and extensive library of templates, images, and fonts make it accessible to both beginners and experienced designers.

Canva's drag-and-drop functionality simplifies the design process, enabling users to produce professional-quality visuals without needing advanced design skills.

Canva takes a more traditional approach to graphic design than DALL-E. Canva provides a structured environment where you can manually design and customize your visuals using preexisting elements. Canva works well for projects that require *precise control* over the design process and use a more *conventional aesthetic.*

Diagrams and Flowcharts

Common diagrams used in education, organizations, teams and other situations include organization charts, flow diagrams, mind maps, Gantt charts, and data visualizations. Unlike illustrations, diagrams require *precision.* These require structure, not creative interpretation.

Next, we'll look at Lucidchart, a software product for diagramming, and two approaches to creating diagrams with ChatGPT: DALL-E and Mermaid.js.

Lucidchart

Lucidchart is a *diagramming tool* designed for creating flowcharts, org charts, mind maps, process diagrams, and technical visuals. Lucidchart focuses on *structure and logic* rather than aesthetics. It's ideal for workflows, decision trees, and system diagrams where clarity and precision matter.

Lucidchart offers a user-friendly, *drag-and-drop* interface with *templates* and *shape libraries* that are often—but not exclusively—used to support business, engineering, and software use cases.

You can easily adjust layout, text, and connections, and the platform supports real-time collaboration. Lucidchart is cloud-based and integrates with tools like Google Drive, Microsoft Office, Slack, and Atlassian.

While Canva is better for polished visuals, Lucidchart excels at logical structure and team-friendly editing. It's a strong choice when you need to map out a process or system clearly and revise it as your thinking evolves.

Diagramming With ChatGPT

ChatGPT can generate clean, attractive diagrams using DALL·E, but they work best when the *structure is simple.*

These diagrams are high-resolution images, *not editable files*. You can't change text or reposition boxes unless you import the image into a graphics tool like Photoshop. Still, if you want a good-looking diagram for a presentation or report, DALL·E is fast and reliable.

If you need precision or expect to revise the diagram, tools like Canva or Lucidchart may be better. They let you adjust text, layout, and formatting with full control.

Another option is to ask ChatGPT to produce the diagram using Mermaid.js.

About Mermaid.js

Mermaid.js is a *plain-text format* for generating diagrams. You can prompt ChatGPT to write Mermaid code, then paste that code into Mermaid Live Editor to generate a diagram. You can export it as a PNG or SVG files. SVG files can be imported into PowerPoint and converted into editable shapes.

This approach gives you *full control.* You can revise the diagram by editing the text. The tradeoff is that Mermaid has its own syntax, which takes a little time to learn.

Here is a prompt for creating an organization chart using ChatGPT and DALL-E:

> **Please create an illustration, 1024×1024, showing an org chart titled 'Leadership Team' with CEO Jordan Lee at the top. Three reports: Head of Marketing (Tina Chen), Head of Product (Marcus Ray), Head of Operations (Dana Scott). Head of Product manages two people: Product Manager (Alex Nguyen) and Development Manager (Priya Patel). Use dark text and clean layout.**

This ChatGPT prompt, using DALL-E, generated the following org chart:

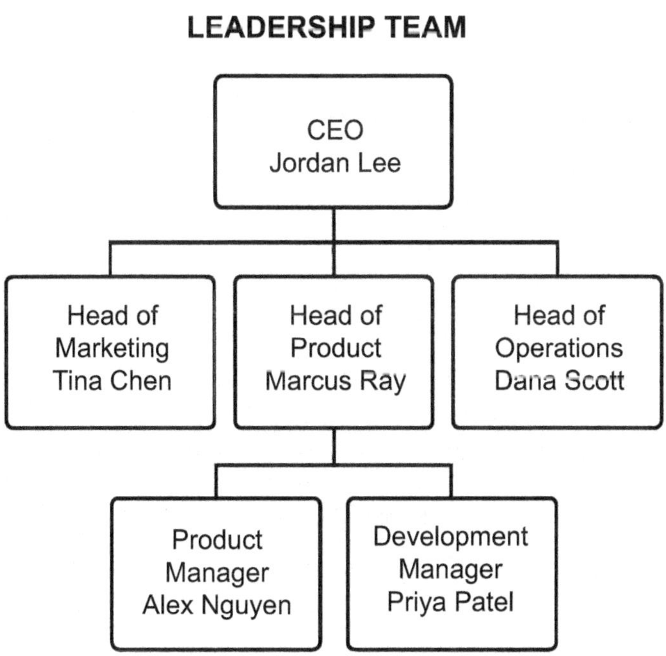

Here is a prompt for creating the same organization chart, instructing ChatGPT to produce it in Mermaid.js format. The output is pasted into the Mermaid Live Editor or another program that converts it to a diagram:

Please use Mermaid.js syntax to generate an org chart titled 'Leadership Team' with CEO Jordan Lee at the top. Three reports: Head of Marketing (Tina Chen), Head of Product (Marcus Ray), Head of Operations (Dana Scott). Head of Product manages two people: Product Manager (Alex Nguyen) and Development Manager (Priya Patel).

ChatGPT can produce mermaid.js output that *describes* a diagram. It doesn't directly generate an image.

The prompt produces Mermaid.js output:

```
%% Leadership Team Org Chart
graph TD
  CEO["CEO<br>Jordan Lee"]
  CEO --> Marketing["Head of Marketing<br>Tina Chen"]
  CEO --> Product["Head of Product<br>Marcus Ray"]
  CEO --> Operations["Head of Operations<br>Dana Scott"]
  Product --> PM["Product Manager<br>Alex Nguyen"]
  Product --> Dev["Development Manager<br>Priya Patel"]
```

You need to paste the Mermaid.js output into the Mermaid Live Editor or another software product to create the diagram as it appears here:

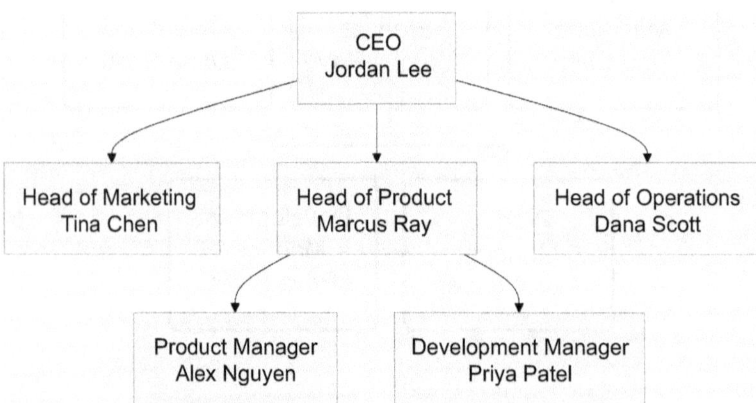

Choosing a Tool for Diagrams

Use **DALL·E:**

- You want a clean, polished image for display.
- The result looks good with minimal effort.
- You don't need to make changes.
- You can't edit the layout or text after it's created.

Use **Mermaid.js:**

- You need a diagram that can be versioned, reused, or updated by editing plain text.
- The output is flexible but not visually refined
- For tech-savvy users or anyone working with Markdown or documentation tools.
- You're comfortable making the effort required to learn the syntax.

Use **Lucidchart or Canva**

- You're a comfortable but not technical user.
- You would like he best mix of control and ease.
- You want full editing control but don't want to deal with diagram syntax or image-generation prompts.
- You want to be able to drag and drop shapes, edit text, adjust layout, and export in multiple formats.

Takeaways for Chapter 13

Visuals enhance the effectiveness and engagement of documents both through decorative illustrations and diagrams that communicate structure and process. Visuals also support storytelling. They make the content more engaging and accessible. AI-generated visuals are high-quality, quick to produce, and affordable, but it can be difficult to get exactly what you envision. AI tools like DALL-E create graphics from text prompts. While AI can generate stunning visuals, its lack of understanding of the physical world can lead to unexpected results.

1. Images, diagrams, and infographics make documents more engaging and easier to understand.
2. They are very effective to quickly and clearly communicate your message to diverse audiences.
3. They are great at building communication and presentation skills in ways you may not have expected, like storytelling or to generate visuals in a variety of ways.
4. Platforms like DALL-E and Canva allow you to create high-quality visuals without needing artistic skills.
5. AI-generated visuals can be unpredictable, requiring refinement and manual corrections.
6. The more detailed and specific your AI prompts, the better the results you'll achieve.
7. AI doesn't understand or experience the real world, which can lead to unexpected results. AI does not "see" objects or visualize them as people would.
8. AI-generated images may need resizing or upscaling to meet print and digital publishing standards.
9. You can use Canva or Lucidchart to create diagrams where you want control and precision. These tools offer drag-and-drop interactions.
10. When you need simple, attractive diagrams for presentations and reports, ChatGPT with DALL-E is a good choice. However, you cannot easily edit the output, so you may need to keep revising your prompts to get what you want.
11. ChatGPT can produce mermaid.js output that describes a diagram. You can input the Mermaid into Mermaid Live Editor or another software product to create the diagram.

PART 5

The Road Ahead

AI is a transformational technology. Its promise is immense, but the future is uncertain. One thing is clear: Learning about AI is not a one-and-done effort. AI is evolving rapidly, and as it becomes embedded in business processes and everyday tools, your needs will keep changing along with the skills you need. At the frontier lies Artificial General Intelligence (AGI), which aims to create systems that reason, adapt, and solve novel problems. Whether AGI is achievable—or what form it might take—remains unknown.

The techniques in this book equip you to manage uncertainty. They strengthen your ability to think critically when information is incomplete or misleading. They build agility, helping you adapt as conditions shift. And they foster continuous learning and effective communication. These are the skills that will keep you adaptable and a step ahead as the future unfolds. To prepare for whatever lies ahead, to stay engaged, keep learning, and develop your own AI fluency. One step at a time.

CHAPTER 14

Finding Your AI Voice

The most durable thing in writing is style.
—George Orwell

In Chapter 13, you saw how adjusting the tone in a prompt can produce a solid draft that you can edit. Asking for something professional and friendly often yields text that, after a little cleanup, works well for routine business writing. Asking for text that is formal and concise works well for policies and procedures.

But sometimes you want the speed of AI-generated text, but with more of your own voice and style. You can get surprisingly close by refining the tone, providing a sample of your writing, and giving ChatGPT a few clear instructions. It's not flawless, but with the right setup, you can produce a draft that needs only light editing and feels more personal than typical AI output.

There are four elements you can tweak:

1. Tone
2. Style
3. A writing sample
4. Constraints

As you work with these, ChatGPT will get better at approximating your voice, especially if you use consistent examples and feedback.

Voice

Your voice as a writer makes your work uniquely yours. Your voice affects how well your writing lands with your audience. It influences clarity, credibility, and alignment with your brand or goals. Voice is shaped by style and tone, two elements that influence how your writing feels to the reader. ChatGPT can adjust both, helping you to produce text that fits your purpose, audience, and personality.

- *Style* is how you express ideas. It includes word choice, sentence structure, and language patterns. It gives your writing its personality.
- *Tone* is your attitude toward the subject or audience: serious, playful, formal, or relaxed. It shapes the mood and emotional impact of your writing.

Style and tone are closely connected, and you don't need to worry too much about separating them. In practice, you can simply specify both in a single prompt. For example, you might ask for a "formal and analytical" explanation, or "friendly and conversational" instructions. You can specify tone and style explicitly in a prompt, context file, or style guide.

As always, experiment to be sure the output fits. For instance, I once asked for a casual explanation of photosynthesis and got: "Hey there! So, photosynthesis is this awesome process where plants turn sunlight into food. Cool, right?" That might work on social media, but not in a college course.

Personal Style and Voice

You can get ChatGPT to approximate your personal voice by uploading a sample of your writing. ChatGPT evaluates a range of features to build a lightweight internal model of your voice and style. The key factors it analyzes are:

- Tone
- Style
- Vocabulary and diction
- Point of view and pronoun use
- Structure and flow
- Level of formality
- Typical sentence patterns

How to Choose Your Sample

Look through your existing writing for patterns, tone, and words you typically use. Provide ChatGPT with samples that clearly showcase this voice. If you consistently reinforce your style preferences through iterative feedback, ChatGPT will continue to refine the model so it gets closer to emulating your own style and tone. However, it may fail to grasp nuances, so some editing will be required.

When choosing your writing sample, select a passage of about 150–300 words that is representative of your desired tone, style, and purpose. Before pasting it in, clean up typos or stray edits, since you don't want these in the model.

Here is a prompt template you can use:

- **I want you to match my writing style.**
- **Here's a sample of my writing:**
- **[paste your sample here—150 to 300 words is enough]**
- **Use the sample to understand how I write.**
- **From now on, write in the same tone and style unless I ask for something different.**

Adding Constraints

You may find that ChatGPT has specific writing quirks that you don't want. You can add constraints to the prompt, telling ChatGPT what to avoid. Here's an example of a prompt that contains constraints. You can alter the conditions to suit your own style:

I want you to match my writing style for future tasks.

Here's a short sample of my writing:

'ChatGPT won't replace your judgment. But it can speed up problem-solving, help you clarify ideas, and be deliberate about the words you choose. As you develop an understanding of how it works, you will become adept at using it, while improving your ability to think critically, and communicate more clearly."

Use this to understand my tone and style. From now on, write in a similar voice unless I ask for something different.

Please also follow these constraints to keep the writing consistent:

- **Use active voice**
- **Keep sentences between 10 and 20 words**

- **Stick to clear, direct language with no jargon**
- **Avoid metaphors, emotional framing, or filler**
- **Use only basic punctuation. Avoid semicolons and em dashes**

By adding constraints to your writing sample, you will get text closer to your own voice.

Assigning Roles to ChatGPT

In Chapter 6, we discussed assigning a role to ChatGPT so it responds with a specific perspective. This technique is also useful when generating text. For example, you could add one of these roles to a prompt:

- **"Imagine you are a college professor teaching an introductory class to non-engineers."**
- **"Assume the role of a supportive mental health counselor helping an anxious person."**
- **"Act as if you were a primary school teacher explaining AI to young children."**

Here's the result of assigning ChatGPT these three roles when asking it to explain AI in 25 words:

Prompt	Output
Imagine you are a college professor teaching an introductory class to non-engineers. Explain what AI is 25 words.	Artificial intelligence (AI) is technology enabling machines to simulate humanlike thinking, learning, and decision making, using data, algorithms, and patterns to solve problems efficiently.
Pretend you are a supportive mental health counselor helping an anxious person. Explain what AI is in 25 words.	AI is a tool that helps machines learn and solve problems, like a helpful assistant, designed to make tasks easier and less stressful.
Act as if you were a primary school teacher explaining AI to young children. Explain what AI is in 25 words.	AI is like teaching computers to think a little bit like people so they can help us do things more easily.

As a longer example of the way styles and tone shapes ChatGPT's output, compare these three 75-word paragraphs generated by this prompt:

Please write a 75-word paragraph on the topic "Why clear communication is essential to good team performance." Produce three versions with different tones: 1-formal and authoritative, 2-informal and friendly, 3-upbeat and funny. Label each version with its tone/style.

This prompt produced the following output, illustrating different tones on the same topic:

Formal and Authoritative
Clear communication is the foundation of effective teamwork. When team members understand expectations, goals, and each other's perspectives, they can coordinate actions efficiently and avoid costly errors. Clear communication fosters trust, minimizes misunderstandings, and accelerates decision-making. It ensures that tasks are executed correctly the first time, reduces duplication of effort, and allows for prompt resolution of issues—ultimately leading to higher performance and better results.

Informal and Friendly
Good communication is like oil in a well-run machine—it keeps everything moving smoothly. When everyone's on the same page, work gets done faster, problems get solved sooner, and people feel more connected. It cuts down on confusion, keeps projects on track, and helps teammates trust and support each other.

Upbeat and Funny
Teamwork without clear communication is like playing charades with blindfolds—lots of wild guesses and not much progress. When people actually share what they mean (and mean what they share), the whole team clicks. Ideas flow, mistakes drop, and suddenly you're winning the game instead of acting it out.

Matching Style and Tone to Your Purpose

Style and tone work best when they match your intent and audience. Here are a few combinations worth trying. See what works best for your project:

You can also try *blending* styles and tones. Here are some examples of combinations you can request:

- **"Use a formal but friendly tone with a mix of expository and narrative styles."**
- **"Write in a concise, technical style with a reassuring tone."**
- **"Use a conversational tone with a persuasive and descriptive style to explain this product."**
- **"Adopt a serious tone with a poetic and lyrical style for a reflective personal essay."**
- **"Combine a satirical tone with a journalistic style to critique current trends."**
- **"Write in a minimalistic style with an inspirational tone for a motivational quote."**

Table 14.1 Useful style and tone combinations

Purpose	Recommended style + tone
Professional report	Analytical or technical + formal or authoritative
Marketing copy	Persuasive + inspirational or optimistic
Internal team update	Conversational + informal or friendly
Blog post (engaging)	Narrative or descriptive + humorous, curious, or whimsical
Executive summary	Direct or analytical + serious or objective
Personal essay or memoir	Evocative or narrative + emotional or reflective
Educational material	Expository or academic + empathetic or encouraging
Creative writing	Lyrical or experimental + romantic, melancholic, or satirical

Layer tones and styles to get the voice you want. It's easy to try different combinations by asking ChatGPT to rewrite a paragraph or two, using a prompt. Experiment, adjust, and revise so you'll learn which combinations work best.

Available Styles and Tones

Below are some common tone and style options. Some are widely useful, others are more specialized. These lists aren't exhaustive; ask ChatGPT for additional suggestions.

Table 14.2 Styles for document types

Style	Definition	Best for
Abstract	Conceptual less grounded in detail	Theoretical writing and philosophy
Academic	Structured and scholarly	Research papers and journal articles
Analytical	Logical and methodical	Reports, essays, and business analysis
Colloquial	Regional and informal	Dialogue, local storytelling, and blogs
Conversational	Friendly and engaging	Emails, casual documents, and blogs
Descriptive	Rich in sensory details	Creative writing, travel, food, and memoir
Direct	Straightforward and to the point	Instructions, user guides, and briefings
Evocative	Emotionally and visually expressive	Essays, branding, and narrative nonfiction
Expository	Informative and explanatory	Tutorials, explainers, and technical
Experimental	Unconventional and innovative	Literary fiction, poetry, and avant-garde
Flowery	Ornate and elaborate	Historical fiction and romantic prose
Gritty	Raw, unpolished, intense	Crime fiction, memoir, and journalism
Journalistic	Factual and concise	News, reports, and documentaries
Lyrical	Musical and expressive	Poetry, fiction, and creative essays
Minimalistic	Simple and understated	Design writing, UX, and modern prose
Narrative	Storytelling	Case studies, fiction, and essays
Persuasive	Arguments and convincing	Marketing, proposals, and opinion pieces
Poetic	Rhythmic and artistic	Poetry, lyrical essays, and literary fiction
Satirical	Mocking and ironic	Commentary, humor writing, and op-eds
Technical	Precise and detailed	Manuals, scientific content, and specs

Common Writing Tones

Table 14.3 Tones for document types

Tone	Definition	Best for
Authoritative	Confident and commanding	Executive reports and formal arguments
Critical	Analytical and judgmental	Reviews, analyses, and academic debate
Curious	Inquisitive and open-minded	Interviews, exploration, and learning blogs
Empathetic	Understanding and compassionate	Health care, coaching, and support material
Emotional	Evocative and heartfelt	Speeches, storytelling, and memoir
Formal	Polished and professional	Business reports, proposals, and academic
Humorous	Funny, lighthearted, or playful	Blogs, creative writing, and speeches
Informal	Casual and conversational	Emails, blogs, and user-friendly content
Inspirational	Uplifting and motivating	Speeches, branding, and self-help
Melancholic	Reflective and somber	Memoir, poetry, and literature
Mystical	Enigmatic and spiritual	Fantasy, poetry, and philosophical writing
Objective	Neutral and factual	Journalism, scientific writing, and legal
Optimistic	Positive and hopeful	Marketing, coaching, and motivational text
Persuasive	Convincing and compelling	Advertising, proposals, and essays
Pessimistic	Negative or skeptical	Editorials, satire, and dystopian writing
Romantic	Passionate and affectionate	Poetry, fiction, and love letters
Sarcastic	Ironic and biting	Satire, commentary, and entertainment
Serious	Straightforward and solemn	Policy, technical writing, and legal
Urgent	Pressing and immediate	Calls to action and crisis communication
Whimsical	Fanciful and imaginative	Children's books and creative writing

Takeaways for Chapter 14

This chapter explores how to shape your writing voice by using style and tone. Style controls your expressive patterns, and tone controls your emotional attitude. The chapter also covers how to upload a writing sample that ChatGPT will use to create a model of your writing to guide text generation. The chapter includes reference tables for common styles and tones and explains how to blend them to get the voice you want. You'll also find practical examples showing how different tones and styles affect the final output.

1. Your writing voice is the unique combination of style and tone that defines how your writing feels and sounds to readers.
2. Style refers to your language patterns: word choice, sentence structure, and expressive techniques. Tone reflects your attitude toward the subject or audience.
3. You can ask ChatGPT to adopt a specific tone or style, or both, using a prompt, a context file, or a style guide.
4. Uploading a writing sample allows ChatGPT to analyze and approximate your personal voice.
5. Assigning roles (e.g., teacher, coach, executive) helps ChatGPT tailor its output to match your audience and purpose.
6. Reference tables for styles and tones can help you identify the best fit for a specific writing task.
7. It's often useful to blend styles and tones, such as combining a persuasive style with an inspirational tone or a conversational tone with a technical style. You can experiment with combinations like "formal and friendly" or "minimalistic and optimistic" to find the voice that best suits your project.

CHAPTER 15

Your AI Journey—From Impact to Insight

By Anne Pauker Kreitzberg

AI is a tool. The choice about how it gets deployed is ours.
—Oren Etzioni

This final chapter focuses on you. We hope that this book has provided a foundation on which you can continue to build skills to support your work and personal growth. In this final chapter, we'll share some ideas about the best ways you can use AI to continue to build your personal and professional work by honing AI literacy to increase the depth and breadth of knowledge and skills that will last a lifetime and expand opportunities for the forseeable future.

Warp Speed and Bumps in the Road

It's hardly news to point out that the path to future success is not clear. AI is expanding at an unprecedented rate. It took 20 years for the personal computer and Internet, and even the cell phone, to become widely adopted. When OpenAI released the first public version of ChatGPT in November 2022, they claimed more than a million users within 5 days and 700 million by 2025—growth that is almost unimaginable.

Many businesses see an opportunity to use AI to increase productivity and reduce costs, but don't yet understand how to accomplish it. At the same time, AI tech companies are fiercely competing for dominance in a future they, too, don't fully agree upon.

This pace of growth is difficult to sustain, and there will be bumps on the road ahead. Many factors remain unclear: the technology itself, the business models around it, how AI will be used to augment work, and the effect it will have. Regulators are slow to act and don't fully understand the technology or the issues, leaving the industry to self-regulate. Bad actors, unchecked greed, the environmental impact of data centers, and the social impact of misinformation are all problems for debate.

There are many risks, but the genie is out of the bottle. AI has enormous potential and promise for improving lives. As a result of the work you have done so far, you have seen AI's strengths and its limitations. You are well-positioned to be a skeptical consumer and contribute your ideas to the conversation.

Is AI Coming for Your Job?

A significant fear is that AI will automate jobs out of existence. Some jobs will disappear, while AI tools will augment others, making them more efficient. Almost every job will be affected in some way. The truth is, no one knows what the future will bring.

What does seem clear is that just as familiarity with Word, PowerPoint, and Excel became a baseline qualification for many jobs, AI literacy will soon be required as well. Your value in the marketplace will be greatest with more than a superficial understanding of AI. You have already started that journey. Every time you're faced with an unfamiliar problem, a new role, or work with new people, you have an opportunity to engage with AI and go deeper.

Future Proof Yourself

Think of yourself as an explorer entering unfamiliar territory. You cannot map every step on your path, but you know you're bound to discover obstacles along the way. Your survival may depend on preparation for a variety of scenarios. This takes anticipation of the types of obstacles you may encounter, awareness of your limitations, and honing skills that will help you adjust to whatever you encounter. You'll be able to "think on the fly," make mid-course corrections, and take advantage of opportunities others might miss.

A Springboard for Business survey (January 2024) found that most leaders ranked critical and strategic thinking as the most important soft skills in today's workforce, yet many also reported these abilities are in short supply. Throughout 2025, the business press, including *The Wall Street Journal* and *The Financial Times*, highlighted the "skills gap" between what is taught in school and the abilities needed in an AI-powered workplace.

This suggests an opportunity to future-proof yourself by using AI to fill these needs.

Use AI Sharpen Future-Proofing Skills

This book has given you techniques to future-proof your skills in an AI-powered workplace, and navigate uncertainty and change.

The techniques built on Guided Q&A are very effective because they walk you through clarifying and solving problems, step by step, and help you plan and rehearse ways to interact constructively with others. Learning in the context of a real problem is one of the most efficient ways to learn or deepen your thinking skills.

This technique is called "Just-in-Time" learning. A huge benefit is that you use it now to expand your ability to be more successful dealing with the issues at hand, which promotes learning, skills and the ability to more confidently adjust to change.

Critical Thinking and AI

Critical thinking, the set of skills most sought by business leaders and in all employment or volunteer situations, is wide-ranging. People recognize its importance but aren't quite clear exactly how to do it.

Critical thinking comprises a set of skills that are the basis for decision making, problem solving, analytical or strategic thinking, and even creativity. We discovered in our work with teams over the past 25 years that these same skills are the foundation for communication and collaboration, as well as agility and adaptability.

The same set of skills is the same; what changes is the purpose to which it's applied. Depending on your job or role, you may not be involved in large-scale strategic thinking or in creative, innovative, or artistic projects. But understanding how and when to apply core critical thinking skills adds considerably to your toolbox in a wide variety of situations. They are the foundation for communication and collaboration, an essential skill for working with other people.

"Agile Thinking" is the application of critical thinking skills that enable you to quickly recognize a change, reconsider a situation, reevaluate assumptions, alternatives, and risk to update your approach as circumstances shift—which they inevitability do.

Critical Thinking Is More Than Logic

Many people think of critical thinking as distinguishing fact from fiction, identifying faulty logic, and weighing alternative options and decisions. These are all components of critical thinking, but not the whole story.

By simple illustration, we see how decisions are made in the stock market; sure, financials are part of the equation, but most experts will tell you that an awful lot of emotion and guesses about the future affect trades.

So how does this affect you?

Clarifying emotions, bias, organizational realities, culture and social dynamics, conflicting assumptions, and risk tolerance are all factors you need to consider when you're thinking about a situation. These factors shape how people understand the situation and the goal. It can be easy to miss that people frequently use the same words, but each may have a very different definition, picture of the situation, solution and how to get it done. Our work with cross-functional teams taught us that this often starts Day One of a project - only to be the root of disagreement, churn and decisions that arise far down the line.. Biases determine the data people trust, how they think about alternatives, and ultimately how decisions are made.

The techniques in Chapter 6 that allow you to rehearse interactive conversations may be particularly helpful here. While you may not always have the subject matter expertise in a particular area, you will be able to work with others who do. You will be able to use ChatGPT to familiarize yourself with the basics you need through Socratic discussion and related techniques like Deep Research and Interactive Q&A.

Use ChatGPT in the Moment

ChatGPT is available everywhere—on your PC, laptop, and phone. You may not always have access to enterprise-specific documents from everywhere, but you can access a massive knowledge base whenever you want. It may be useful for you to keep a set of favorite prompts readily available (as a Word, or Google Docs file, or on your phone) so you can copy and paste them into ChatGPT on the go.

Here are examples of common work situations where you can apply ChatGPT techniques, either to prepare or use in the moment:

- You're working on a project, use ChatGPT to research how others have approached similar problems.
- Ask ChatGPT to highlight common pitfalls and help you surface assumptions that might not be explicit.
- You're at a meeting and hear something you're not sure is correct. Use ChatGPT to quickly check it.
- Suggest a tactful way to question comments made without derailing the discussion.
- You want to make a suggestion you feel strongly about and present it so people will consider it seriously rather than dismiss it out of hand.
- Use ChatGPT to draft versions to engage others in conversation.
- You're asked to propose a recommendation and want to be able to defend it. Use ChatGPT to help you frame the proposal and prepare you for counter-arguments.
- You are preparing for a meeting that might get contentious. One person tends to dominate the discussion. Use ChatGPT to: role-play the conversation, generate respectful phrases to redirect focus without escalating conflict, and practice responses that keep the discussion productive.

Asking the right questions, actively looking for opposing points of view, helping you craft communications, and becoming more agile will make you more informed, open to exploring new ideas and perspectives, and credible. These are among the most powerful capabilities of generative AI. And everything you need in order to take advantage of this is right at your fingertips 24/7/365.

Stay Curious

Walt Disney credited curiosity for his success when he said, "We keep moving forward, opening new doors and doing new things, because we're curious."

The strongest motivation to learn is curiosity. Children learn by asking "why" again and again, quickly absorbing what they hear, often in imaginative ways. Adults don't always make time for thinking, wondering, or daydreaming.

AI gives you an opportunity to boost your curiosity. It makes it easy to play out new ideas, "what ifs" and see things through different eyes. Whether it's digging deeper or exploring topics you've been curious about but never get to, continuous learning is one of the most important things you can do to stay relevant and adapt in an AI-Powered Workplace.

It provides you with an amazing, readily accessible opportunity to learn, expand your beliefs and enlarge your world in ways that may not have seemed as relevant or applicable while you were in school. It makes you more prepared, capable, open to change, and better able to collaborate with others. It's a winning strategy that holds its value over time.

What's Next?

This book has given you practical techniques, mental models, and real-world prompts to guide your personal AI journey. Follow them, practice, and proceed with confidence, creativity, and care.

As your work evolves, return to these tools with fresh perspectives. You'll discover new possibilities as well as new challenges. That is the nature of learning in a time of rapid change, uncertainty, and complexity.

We wish you an exciting journey as you use AI to reach your fullest potential. Stay curious. Be constructive. Be ethical. And always remain human.

PART 6

Dig Deeper

This appendix contains resources and reference materials for those who want to dig more deeply into ChatGPT.

In this part, you will find four sections:

1. Project Ideas
2. Creative Writing
3. Glossary of AI Terms
4. References and Inspiration

Project Ideas

This section suggests ideas for projects to explore working with using AI.

Blog Post Introduction

Draft an engaging introduction for a blog post on the benefits of remote work. Use a conversational but professional tone. Include one statistic.

Brand Story

Craft a short brand story for a sustainable furniture startup. Show values through a customer's perspective. Keep under 200 words.

Educational Infographic

Write a concise text for an infographic on the water cycle for middle school students. Use clear headings and short sentences.

FAQ Section

Draft three FAQs and answers for a startup offering AI-driven marketing. Keep answers under 50 words, clear and jargon-free.

Interview Questions

Generate five thoughtful interview questions for a social media manager. Focus on strategy, analytics, and creative execution.

Newsletter Update

Write a 120-word newsletter update about a new software feature. Use bullet points for highlights.

Press Release

Write a press release for a new electric bike. Emphasize eco-benefits, affordability, and urban commuting. Keep under 400 words.

Product Description

Write a 100-word description of a smartwatch. Emphasize health features, design, and emotional appeal. Provide three alternate versions: technical, lifestyle, and aspirational.

Proposal Summary

Draft a one-paragraph executive summary for a CRM proposal. Focus on efficiency, ROI, and implementation timeline.

Social Media Ad Copy

Write three versions of an Instagram ad for a new organic skincare line. Make one playful, one elegant, and one data-driven.

Speech Outline

Generate an outline for a 3-minute speech on cybersecurity in small businesses. Include a hook, three key points, and a closing call to action.

Survey Questions

Generate five survey questions on delivery and product quality. Avoid using "and" or "or" to ensure you survey one dimension. Use neutral, non-leading language.

Travel Guide

Write a 200-word travel guide for first-time visitors to Tokyo. Include three must-see spots, food tips, and one cultural insight.

Tutorial Outline

Create a five-step outline for setting up a LinkedIn profile. Target recent graduates. Include what not to do.

Video Script

Write a 60-second YouTube script explaining how to use a personal finance app. Use a clear structure: hook, demo, benefits, and close.

Project Ideas Using Websites

You can paste live links directly into your prompt. The model can open and summarize them. You can adapt them to run periodically by defining an *agent* (see Chapter 5).

Summarize a Webpage

Summarize this article [insert link]. Focus on the main arguments and supporting evidence.>Extract Structured Data

From this product page [insert link], extract product names, prices, and descriptions in a table.

Compare Multiple Sources

Compare these two articles [insert link1] and [insert link2]. Summarize key differences in tone, evidence, and conclusions.

Analyze Writing Style

Analyze the writing style of this blog [insert link]. Describe tone, sentence structure, and engagement techniques.

Validate Information

Check if this article [insert link] supports or contradicts the claim: "Remote work increases productivity by 25%.

Creative Writing

Fiction is not the focus of this book, and the stories you generate with ChatGPT will not be as engaging as those written by professional authors. A strong story depends on vision, emotional nuance, and irony. These are areas where large language models fall short.

Still, stories can be powerful tools for communication. They grab attention, illustrate points, create relatable scenarios, and are memorable. Stories strengthen speeches, presentations, training, and marketing.

While ChatGPT should not write your novel, it can produce short, engaging pieces if you plan carefully and give clear input. You need to define characters, context, and emotional stakes. You should also edit the output to add human resonance.

Vague prompts produce generic stories. Detailed prompts with emotional cues and inner thoughts yield better results.

Example 1: A Simple Prompt

Write a 150-word story about a family who had to migrate due to climate change.

> The Hassan family had lived by the sea for generations. Fishing was their rhythm, until the tides betrayed them. Each year, storms grew fiercer. The shoreline shrank. Their home stood one cyclone away from ruin.
>
> When the final storm swept it away, they packed what they could carry. Ahmed, the eldest, found factory work in the city. "This is not the life I studied for," he thought. His sister Aisha missed the sound of waves. "Why is the city so loud, and why can't I sleep?"
>
> Their parents tried to be strong, but each night Meena whispered, "Will we ever belong here?"
>
> They clung to hope, dreaming of a return. But the sea, once their provider, had become their loss.

This is readable but still limited. A stronger prompt creates richer conflict and more emotional depth.

Example 2: A More Detailed Prompt

Write a 150-word story about the Patel family, rice farmers who had to migrate when climate change caused alternating drought and floods. The goal is to show the human cost of climate change. Write in a creative, emotional style. Include the inner thoughts and feelings of each family member: a father, a mother, a teenage son losing his dream of college, and a 9-year-old daughter who must leave her favorite tree. Show how they cope.

The Patels had coaxed rice from their fields for generations. Then the rains betrayed them—first drowning their seedlings, then abandoning them to cracked soil. By the third failed harvest, silence replaced hope.

Arun no longer walked the paddies at dawn. "What good is dawn when nothing grows?" Meena forced strength for the children, though her eyes searched endlessly. "How do I keep us whole?"

Rohan, sixteen, folded his college brochures. "Dreams are for others now," he told himself, taking night shifts instead. Nine-year-old Anjali hugged her banyan tree. "Please wait for me," she whispered through tears.

In the crowded shelter, grief pressed in. Yet small acts helped: Meena cooked for other families, Arun fixed broken latches, Rohan taught Anjali math, sketching trees in the margins. They carried loss, but endured—together.

This version feels more human because the characters reveal their inner lives, but the story could be improved.

Sample Prompts for Business Storytelling

Marketing and Branding

Write a short story that illustrates the value of our service for small business owners. Make it relatable, realistic, and emotionally engaging. Include inner thoughts so the customer feels real.

Create a story about a fictional client who overcame a business challenge using our consulting framework. Keep it under 300 words, hopeful in tone, and show the client's doubts and decisions.

Training and Development

Develop a story about a new team leader learning to give constructive feedback. Make it realistic for corporate training. Show the leader's inner struggle and small victories.

Write a narrative for time-management training. The protagonist should feel overwhelmed, think through the stress internally, and discover a simple, effective strategy.

Internal Communication and Change Management

Tell a story about a company adopting new software. Use a tone that's reassuring and practical. Include employees' initial doubts and gradual acceptance through inner dialog.

Presentations and Speaking Engagements

Create a short parable (under 200 words) on strategic focus. Give the protagonist a clear thought process that guides their choice. Keep it timeless.

Glossary of AI Terms

Term	Definition
AGI (Artificial General Intelligence)	A current research priority to create AI systems capable of reasoning and problem-solving in any domain.
API (Application Programming Interface)	A programming interface provided by OpenAI, allowing developers to integrate models like ChatGPT into applications.
Artificial Intelligence (AI)	A field of computer science focused on creating systems capable of performing tasks requiring human intelligence, such as language understanding, decision making, and problem-solving.
Bias	Systematic tendencies in AI responses resulting from biases present in training data, potentially affecting the accuracy and fairness of outputs.
Brainstorming	Using ChatGPT to generate ideas, explore problems from multiple angles, analyze arguments, and perform preliminary research. Often results in an outline or summary.
Casual Document	A document generated quickly and distributed with minimal editing, typically conveying timely and relevant but not high-impact information.
Context File	A document specifying a project's purpose, audience, goals, style, and length, providing guidelines to help ChatGPT produce focused, relevant responses.
Context Package	A set of documents that may include a context file, style guide, and reference files, used to guide ChatGPT in generating consistent outputs.
Context Window	The amount of text (measured in *tokens*) the model can consider at one time to generate a coherent response.
Crafted Document	A carefully refined, high-impact document whose content requires precise wording. It can be short (policy or mission statement), long-form (book or white paper), or part of a series.
Embedding	A numerical representation of words or phrases, allowing models to understand semantic relationships and similarities.
Fine-Tuning	An additional training stage where a pretrained model is further refined for specific tasks or domains using specialized datasets.

Term	Definition
Hallucination	When the AI generates plausible-sounding but factually incorrect or nonsensical information, often due to overgeneralizing learned patterns.
Inference	The process of generating outputs or predictions from a trained model based on new input data.
Knowledge Base	ChatGPT's foundational knowledge derived from extensive pretraining on vast datasets, represented mathematically to capture relationships between words and concepts.
Large Language Model (LLM)	An AI model trained on extensive datasets to understand and produce human-like text. Examples include ChatGPT and Gemini.
Neural Network	A neural network is a software structure that learns patterns in data over time, improving as it gets feedback about its predictions.
Overfitting	A situation in which the model learns the training data too closely, diminishing its effectiveness when presented with new, unseen data.
Pretraining	The initial training phase where the model learns broad patterns and language structures from massive datasets.
Prompt	A user-provided input or instruction guiding the AI's response. Effective prompts lead to high-quality outputs.
Reference File	Documents such as articles, manuals, or websites specifically provided by the user for inclusion in AI-generated responses, for example, a company's HR manual or mission statement.
Stop Sequence	A signal used to instruct the AI to end text generation at a specific point.
Style	The distinctive way language is used, determined by word choice, sentence structure, and overall expression.
Temperature	A parameter controlling the randomness of AI responses; lower values yield focused outputs; higher values encourage creativity and variety.
Token	A unit of text (word or part of a word) processed by the AI model. Models use tokens to understand and generate language.
Tone	The attitude or emotional quality conveyed in writing, such as humorous, formal, persuasive, or informative, influencing how material is perceived by the audience.
Training	The process of teaching an AI model using extensive datasets. Can involve *supervised* learning (with labeled data) and *unsupervised* learning (without labels).

Term	Definition
Transformer	A neural network architecture enabling efficient, context-aware language processing and text generation, foundational to large language models like GPT-5.
Voice	The unique combination of style and tone that makes a writer's work distinctive and recognizable.
Zero-shot Learning	The ability of a model to perform *tasks without explicit prior training* on them, relying instead on generalized understanding acquired during pretraining.

References and Inspiration

Agrawal, Ajay, Joshua Gans, and Avi Goldfarb. 2018. Prediction Machines: The Simple Economics of Artificial Intelligence. Boston: Harvard Business Review Press. Reframes AI as an efficiency-enhancing prediction tool and unpacks the economic implications of its falling cost.

Christian, Brian. 2020. The Alignment Problem: Machine Learning and Human Values. New York: W. W. Norton & Company. A deeply human-centered exploration of the challenges in ensuring AI systems reflect and respect human ethics and objectives.

Couric, Katie. 2025. "The 'Godfather of AI,' Dr. Geoffrey Hinton, on AI's Existential Risk." YouTube, August 27. https://youtu.be/NnA2OoH_NFY Geoffrey Hinton, the "godfather of AI" discusses the risks and suggests solutions with veteran journalist Katie Couric.

De Cremer, David. 2024. The AI-Savvy Leader: Nine Ways to Take Back Control and Make AI Work for You. Boston: Harvard Business Review Press. Offers nine practical strategies to help leaders ethically integrate AI as a tool for empowerment rather than disruption.

Eagleman, David. March 10, 2025. "What's the Future of Education in an AI World? (Part 1)." Inner Cosmos with David Eagleman, episode 95. https://www.youtube.com/watch?v=T5UgWryTe6U. Neuroscientist David Eagleman uses his accessible podcast and video series to examine how AI intersects with learning, cognition, and human potential.

Gibbs, Jordan. June 13, 2025. "This Prompt Fools Every AI Detector." Medium. https://medium.com/@jordan_gibbs/this-prompt-fools-every-ai-detector-b9ad8c97c07d. Explains prompt engineering tricks and their implications for the reliability of AI-generated content detection.

Financial Times. September 2, 2025. "AI Is Reshaping Workforce Training and Widening the Skills Gap." *Financial Times*. https://www.washingtonpost.com/business/2025/09/02/ai-skills-jobs-tips/. Coverage of the skills gap in the workforce.

Kislev, Elyakim. 2022. Relationships 5.0: How AI, VR, and Robots Will Reshape Our Emotional Lives. New York: Oxford University Press. Sociologically examines how emerging technologies are transforming the way humans relate emotionally to one another.

Mitchell, Melanie. 2019. Artificial Intelligence: A Guide for Thinking Humans. New York: Farrar, Straus and Giroux. A clear, critically balanced overview of AI's real capabilities, limitations, and prospects—free from technical jargon.

Mollick, Ethan. 2023. Co-Intelligence: Living and Working with AI. New York: Portfolio. Encourages treating AI as a collaborative partner, offering grounded advice on "bringing AI to the table" in work and life.

Narayanan, Arvind, and Sayash Kapoor. 2024. AI Snake Oil: What Artificial Intelligence Can Do, What It Can't, and How to Tell the Difference. Princeton, NJ: Princeton University Press. Debunks AI hype by examining its realistic potential versus common overstatements, with eye-opening case studies.

Olson, Parmy. 2024. Supremacy: AI, ChatGPT and the Race That Will Change the World. New York: St. Martin's Press. A fast-paced narrative about the global competition in generative AI, detailing the rivalry between OpenAI and DeepMind.

Rosso, Cami. 2025. "AI Scientists May Have Discovered LLMs' Light-Bulb Moment." Psychology Today, August 31, 2025. A non-technical discussion of the research that suggests at a certain point, AI moves past simple word analysis to a more conceptual understanding of knowledge.

Shneiderman, Ben. 2022. Human-Centered AI. Oxford: Oxford University Press. Proposes a framework where AI is designed to augment human intelligence, emphasizing trust, transparency, and accountability.

Tegmark, Max. 2017. Life 3.0: Being Human in the Age of Artificial Intelligence. New York: Alfred A. Knopf. A sweeping investigation into how advanced AI could shape the future of work, governance, warfare, and human civilization.

Vaswani, Ashish, Noam Shazeer, Niki Parmar, Jakob Uszkoreit, Llion Jones, Aidan N. Gomez, Łukasz Kaiser, and Illia Polosukhin. 2017. "Attention Is All You Need." Advances in Neural Information Processing Systems 30. https://arxiv.org/abs/1706.03762. The groundbreaking scientific paper introducing the Transformer architecture that enabled today's generative AI.

Wall Street Journal. September 2, 2025. "Companies Struggle to Train Young Employees in AI Skills." Wall Street Journal. https://www.wsj.com/lifestyle/careers/ai-training-young-employees-ed08cedc Coverage that discusses the AI skills gap in the current workforce.

From the first day we started this book, Generative AI has continually evolved, adding new features and capabilities. Rather than update this list at completion, we decided it would be most effective to find, vet, and review new research and resources at our website **agilethinking.com**. We hope you will connect and reach out to us with recommendations of your own.

—Charlie and Anne Kreitzberg

About the Author

Charles Kreitzberg brings together the perspectives of a cognitive psychologist, musician, technologist and UX designer. A chance encounter as a teenager in the 1960s sparked a life-long fascination with the power of technology to enhance human thinking. That insight shaped a six-decade career in programming and product design, speaker and advocate for the UX profession. In 1982, he founded Cognetics, an award-winning UX design consultancy, creating frameworks, tools and techniques adopted worldwide. In 2016, he joined Princeton University as Senior UX Advisor. Charlie's collaborative, practical approach blends humanistic values with technical depth, helping people use digital tools to think more clearly and work more effectively.

Index

Note: Page numbers followed by t refers to tables.